WHICH RELATIONSHIPS BETWEEN CHURCHES AND THE EUROPEAN UNION?

THOUGHTS FOR THE FUTURE

QUELLES RELATIONS ENTRE LES EGLISES ET L'UNION EUROPEENNE?

JALONS POUR L'AVENIR

KATHOLIEKE UNIVERSITEIT LEUVEN
Faculteit Kerkelijk Recht
Faculty of Canon Law

WHICH RELATIONSHIPS BETWEEN CHURCHES AND THE EUROPEAN UNION?

THOUGHTS FOR THE FUTURE

QUELLES RELATIONS ENTRE LES EGLISES ET L'UNION EUROPEENNE

JALONS POUR L'AVENIR

Hans-Joachim KIDERLEN
Heidrun TEMPEL
Rik TORFS

UITGEVERIJ PEETERS
LEUVEN
1995

C.I.P. Koninklijke Bibliotheek Albert I

ISBN 90-6831-754-7 (Peeters Leuven)
ISBN 2-87723-278-6 (Peeters France)
D.1995/0602/101

© 1995 Uitgeverij Peeters, Bondgenotenlaan 153, B-3000 Leuven (Belgium)

CONTENTS
TABLE DES MATIERES

TOWARDS A COMMON LEGAL CONCEPT FOR THE RELATION BETWEEN CHURCHES AND STATE WITH RESPECT TO THE EUROPEAN UNION

Hans-Joachim KIDERLEN

When officials of the established German churches, protestant as well as roman-catholic, think of the European Union, they do this with some anxiety. They feel concerned regarding the future of church-state law in Germany coming under increasing pressure from European legal developments. When a representative of French churches, catholics included, thinks of the EU, he or she might feel much concerned about the preeminence of economic considerations in the construction of Europe, but there will be little complaints about non-existant legal relations between the churches and the Community.

Talking about church-state law on the European level, more exactly the EU level, however is of interest not only because of these differences in perception of the necessity of a particular legal status for the churches, due mostly to historical, social and cultural reasons. All churches in the EU indeed entertain longstanding legal relations, be it of very different sorts, with their respective states. A European Union on its way to statehood of some special kind will have to decide which sort of relations will be the most appropriate for itself, in order to live up to common European constitutional thinking and to secure the respect and cooperation of the churches. However, unlike its mostly very old member states, the EU in modern Europe has to handle from its beginnings many religious communities claiming different rights and traditions. Already now the EU deals with religion, as it is bound by the fundamental right of the freedom of conscience, and as it acts on religious communities, when its legislation, mostly indirectly, has a clear bearing on their activities in matters of fiscality, labour relations, education, and others.

The churches and religious communities, to different degrees, want security of tenure also over against the EU, and acceptance as institutions in the ongoing socio-political dialogue with and within the European Union. The churches, although active in the European public arena together with other actors, claim the respect of the European institutions for being different, sometimes in the name of traditions and rights, and always in the name of their specific message and mandate. The not so new discussion about a constitution for the EU, and the forthcoming Intergovernmental Conference on revision of the Maastricht Treaty, adds to the actuality of these questions.

Wishing to escape the narrow passages of official views and well considered concerns a small informal group of interested lawyers and scholars, using some facilities of the Faculty of Canon Law of the Catholic University of Leuven, and of the Brussels Office of the Evangelical Church in Germany (EKD), met without any official mandate on 3 February 1995 in Brussels for a one day seminar. They were looking for possible aspects of a common concept of state-church law with respect to the EU.

The work of this little seminary was divided into four chapters. As starting points for the debate about the institutional position of the churches and religious communities in the EU the fundamental rights approach, the option of church-state treaties or concordates with the EU, and a cooperative approach for instance by introducing a provision in the Treaty on European Union were analysed as possible options.

Then some effort was given to a synthetic analysis of the main different national models of church-state relations practised in member states of the European Union.

Thirdly Community law was screened to look for the characteristics of already existing relations of the EU with churches and religious communities and of impacts of European law on activities of the churches.

Finally attention was drawn to current areas of socio-political interaction between religious communities and the EU.

Searching for a common concept of law which might rule future church-state relations in the EU, as it turned out, is a twofold exercise. If already now the EU directly or indirectly relates to churches and religious communities and deals with religion, it is a matter of form and constitutional systematics, in what ways the European Union and the churches and religious communities should organize these relations. The Intergovernmental Conference of the EU in 1996 may offer an opportunity to address this issue. On the other hand, and may be more important, the churches in particular have to consider content and substance of their relations with the EU. Do they want to make use of their oecumenical experiences and achievements of the past decades in Europe - and beyond -, in order to play an active role in the building of a European civil society? Or do they first want to clarify their possible specific impact on European unification following their different confessional and national concepts of church-state relations?

The churches and religious communities certainly should as institutions have a specific institutional impact on the development of the EU. However they might be more likely to gain such an impact, if they subordinate their claim to rights and traditions in the European area, still unfamiliar to most of them, to their readyness to become part of the dynamics of European unity and real European players.

VERS UNE POSITION INSTITUTIONNELLE DES EGLISES DANS L'UNION EUROPEENNE.

L'APPROCHE PAR LES DROITS FONDAMENTAUX, L'APPROCHE CONCORDATAIRE ET L'APPROCHE COOPERATRICE

Heidrun TEMPEL

I. L'approche par les droits fondamentaux

La liberté religieuse et la liberté de conscience sont des éléments-clé dans une approche par les droits fondamentaux. Elles représentent le lien entre les différentes constitutions des états membres de l'Union Européenne.

Il faut constater qu'à cause de circonstances historiques et de traditions diverses en Europe, certaines confessions majoritaires ont des relations priviligiées avec l'état, c'est le cas par exemple de l'église orthodoxe en Grèce (cfr. article 3, article 13 «liberté de la confession religieuse»), de l'église catholique en Italie (cfr. article 7, «liberté de la confession religieuse», art. 8), en Irlande où l'église catholique encadre le système constitutionnel et la société, ou encore des églises luthériennes en Scandinavie.

Quelques constitutions nationales font une distinction entre le droit individuel de la pratique religieuse du croyant et les droits corporatifs des communautés religieuses comme le règlement et l'administration libre des affaires du culte.

1. La Convention Européenne des Droits de l'Homme (CEDH) est une base commune des traditions constitutionnelles. Dans le contexte qui nous intéresse, les deux articles suivants sont d'un intérêt essentiel:
Tout d'abord, l'article 9 stipule:

> «Toute personne a droit à la liberté de pensée, de conscience et de religion; ce droit implique la liberté de changer de religion ou de conviction, ainsi que la liberté de manifester sa religion ou sa conviction individuellement ou collectivement, en public ou en privé, par le culte, l'enseignement, les pratiques et l'accomplissement des rites.»

Ensuite, il y a l'article 14:

> «*La jouissance des droits et libertés reconnus dans la présente Convention doit être assurée, sans distinction aucune, fondée notamment sur le sexe, la race, la couleur, la langue, la religion, les opinions politiques ou toutes autres opinions, l'origine nationale ou sociale, l'appartenance à une minorité nationale, la fortune, la naissance ou toute autre situation.*»

qui garantit les droits et libertés de la Convention sans distinction de sexe, de race, de couleur, de langue, de religion, de conviction politique ou autre, d'origine nationale ou de minorité nationale.

L'article 9 accorde un droit positif, tandis que l'article 14 interdit la discrimination et accorde une protection.

Il est reconnu dans la doctrine et la jurisprudence que l'article 9, paragraphe 1, est conçu comme un droit fondamental individuel. Mais il existe des opinions diverses quant à savoir si l'article 9 garantit en outre le droit corporatif des communautés religieuses.[1] La plupart des commentaires de la Convention ne se prononcent pas sur cette question.

La Commission de la CEDH, après avoir fait quelques pas dans cette direction, a constaté qu'une église ou communauté religieuse en tant qu'institution peut se référer à la liberté religieuse exprimée par l'article 9.[2] Cette jurisprudence de la Commission est basée sur l'article 25 de la Convention qui accepte des requêtes introduites par les personnes tant physiques que juridiques.

> «*La Commission peut être saisie d'une requête adressée au Secrétariat Général du Conseil de l'Europe par toute personne physique, toute organisation non gouvernementale ou tout groupe de particuliers, qui se prétend victime d'une violation par l'une des Hautes Parties contractantes des droits reconnus dans la présente Convention, dans le cas où la Haute Partie contractante mise en cause a déclaré reconnaître la compétence de la Commission dans cette matière. Les Hautes Parties contractantes ayant souscrit une telle déclaration s'engagent à n'entraver par aucune mesure l'exercice efficace de ce droit.*»

Récemment la Cour Européenne des Droits de l'Homme a reconnu la qualité d'organisations non-gouvernementales dans le sens de l'article 25 de la Convention, des monastères en Grèce en disant qu'ils relèvent de la tutelle — spirituelle — de l'archevêque du lieu où ils se trouvent et non de celle de l'Etat. Les monastères constituent des entités

---

[1] Blum, *Die Gedanken-, Gewissens- und Religionsfreiheit nach Art. 9 der Europäischen Menschenrechtskonvention*, Berlin 1990, p. 170; Robbers, *Handbuch des Staatskirchenrechts der Bundesrepublik Deutschland*, Berlin 1994, pp. 316.

[2] EMRK, E du 5.5.1979 (Bnr. 7805/77) dans DR 16, 68.

distinctes de ce dernier, à l'égard duquel ils jouissent d'une autonomie complète.[3]

L'article 25 garantit uniquement un droit de procédure et n'implique pas de garanties matérielles. L'article 9 pour sa part implique le droit à la constitution de communautés religieuses et par conséquent le droit à organiser librement les structures et les organes, les compétences et les procédures.

Mais les organes de la Convention (Commission et Cour) n'ont jamais explicitement examiné cet aspect corporatif-individuel de la liberté de religion. Dans le cas Rommelfanger, la Commission ne s'est pas prononcée à ce sujet.[4]

D'après la majorité des auteurs l'article 9 ne constitue qu'un droit purement individuel. Ils justifient cette opinion en argumentant que les pays signataires de la Convention avec leurs traditions très différentes, n'ont pas eu l'intention de changer les relations entre les églises et l'état, telles qu'elles existaient dans chaque pays.

D'autre part, l'interprétation corporatiste de l'article 9 susciterait de graves problèmes pour certaines églises. Ce serait le cas de la Suède, du Danemark et de la Finlande, parce que l'autonomie des églises exige une certaine séparation de l'état.

Pour conclure, la doctrine admet unanimement que l'article 9 de la CEDH accorde la liberté de religion à l'individu mais l'existence d'un droit corporatif reste à discuter.

2. Le problème de l'interprétation de l'article 9 est fondamental pour mes réflexions suivantes:

La CEDH a un double effet juridique. D'abord elle lie les états signataires (le Royaume Uni n'a pas incorporé la CEDH dans le droit national). Ensuite elle a des répercussions au niveau de la Communauté et l'Union Européenne.

Quoique le texte constitutif ne contient pas d'obligation dans ce sens, la Cour des Communautés Européennes a appliqué la Convention comme la «loi fondamentale» de la Communauté. Dans sa jurisprudence elle a développé un système des droits de l'homme. Jusqu'aujourd'hui la liberté religieuse n'a fait qu'une seule fois l'objet d'un litige, à savoir l'action intentée contre la Commission Européenne par un candidat juif à un concours (cas Prais)[5].

---

[3] Cour Européenne des Droits de l'Homme, Arrêt dans l'affaire "Les Saints Monastères en Grèce", du 9.12.1994.

[4] EMRK, E du 6.9.1989 (Bnr. 12242/86 - Rommelfanger/BRD).

[5] EuGH, Rs. 130/75 (Prais/Rat) édition 1976, p. 1589.

Le traité de l'Union Européenne a intégré expressément la Convention des droits de l'homme dans l'ordre juridique communautaire. L'article F, paragraphe 2, impose à l'Union le respect des droits fondamentaux garantis par la Convention et par les traditions constitutionnelles communes comme principes généraux du droit communautaire.

> *«L'union respecte les droits fondamentaux tels qu'ils sont garantis par la Convention européenne de sauvegarde des droits de l'homme et des libertés fondamentales signée à Rome le 4 novembre 1950, et tels qu'ils résultent des traditions constitutionelles communes aux Etats membres, en tant que principes généraux du droit communautaire.»*

Cette référence aux constitutions des états membres, liée à l'obligation de l'Union de respecter l'identité nationale (cfr. article F.1), crée un obstacle aux interventions de la Communauté.

En outre, l'article K.2 impose aux états membres le respect des principes de la CEDH en matière de collaboration intergouvernementale, d'asile, de migration, de lutte contre les stupéfiants, etc.

Pour l'instant on ne peut pas prévoir comment la Cour jugera d'une requête introduite par une communauté religieuse, sur la base de l'article 9 de la CEDH. Une telle question ne pourrait faire l'objet d'une requête que si une matière visée par le traité est en cause.

Cela paraît peu probable en matière de culte et de liturgie. Dans l'exercice de missions pastorales, par exemple dans les hôpitaux ou les jardins d'enfants, gérées par les églises, celles-ci offrent des services qui selon les termes du traité entrent en concurrence avec le secteur privé.

Les services à intérêt public des églises, inspirés par la conviction chrétienne, n'ont jamais été reconnus comme des activités qui se situent en dehors du droit communautaire, dans la mesure ou ces services rendus par les églises ou par leurs organisations diaconales ou caritatives jouiraient d'une exemption des règlements communautaires.

Pour citer un débat actuel — si les églises parvenaient à faire inclure un paragraphe sur l'échange de données à caractère personnel entre les états membres et les communautés religieuses dans le cadre de leurs garanties constitutionnelles nationales dans le préambule de la directive visant la protection des données à caractère personnel, cela présenterait une première reconnaissance des églises et des communautés religieuses en tant qu'institutions et porteuses de droits corporatifs au niveau du droit communautaire secondaire.

3. Au niveau communautaire le respect des droits de l'homme n'est pas satisfaisant. Pour élargir la base de la CEDH dans le droit commu-

nautaire, *l'adhésion des Communautés Européennes* à la CEDH est proposée et discutée depuis plusieurs années.

Le Parlement Européen s'est déclaré largement en faveur de cette adhésion parce que la Communauté en tant que communauté de droit et personne juridique exige un encadrement et l'inclusion dans un système de contrôle et de sanctions en cas d'infractions.[6] Un tel système de protection devrait être accessible à chaque citoyen dans l'Union Européenne.

Un argument important du rapport de la commission juridique du parlement tient compte du fait que la Communauté réglemente beaucoup de matières sensibles qui touchent aux droits fondamentaux de ses citoyens comme par exemple:
– la protection des données à caractère personnel
– le droit de l'environnement
– l'immigration, l'asile et l'expulsion
– la publicité et l'information
– le droit au travail et à la formation professionnelle
– la recherche biotechnologique et biomédicale
– l'égalité des sexes.

Cette liste énumérant quelques domaines d'intervention possibles nous amène à la question de savoir qui agit à l'égard du citoyen et qui est responsable envers lui.

La CEDH offre une protection aux citoyens contre les actions des états signataires.

La Communauté n'est pas un état mais elle est bien une personne juridique (cfr. l'article 210) et elle dispose d'un pouvoir législatif. Ses actes législatifs ont des effets directs pour les citoyens par la voie des règlements qui sont obligatoires dans tous leurs éléments et qui sont directement applicables dans tous les Etats membres (cfr. l'article 189, paragraphe 2) et par des directives qui contiennent des avantages pour les citoyens (*Drittwirkung von Richtlinien*). Mais sans l'adhésion de la Communauté à la CEDH, les institutions de la Communauté ne sont pas directement liées par cette Convention. Même si l'Union s'engage dans l'article F, paragraphe 2, à respecter les droits fondamentaux tels qu'ils sont garantis par la Convention européenne, les citoyens ne peuvent pas porter plainte contre les actions des institutions de l'Union en tant que telles.

---

[6] Rapport de la Commission juridique du Parlement (Bontempi) A3-0421/93 du 8.12.1994; déclaration du Parlement Européen, Bulletin officiel (44/32 du 14.2.1994).

L'adhésion aurait de lourdes conséquences pour la Cour elle-même. Par exemple comment procéder avec les renvois préjudiciels (cfr. l'article 177)? Est-ce qu'un tel renvoi pourra être envoyé à la Commission à Strasbourg *avant* le jugement de la Cour si cela concerne la CEDH ou est-ce qu'une requête sera possible par après?

Dans ce contexte il ne faut pas oublier qu'actuellement tous les Etats membres du Conseil de l'Europe sont invités à signer le protocole d'amendement n° 11 de la Convention par lequel une Cour permanente à deux instances sera créée pour remplacer la Commission et la Cour actuelle.

Est-ce que l'adhésion de la Communauté Européenne rendra superflue l'élaboration par la Communauté elle-même d'un catalogue de droits fondamentaux?

Le Parlement préconise une combinaison de l'adhésion à la CEDH et de la rédaction d'un catalogue de droits fondamentaux par la Communauté. Dans son rapport, il cite l'ex-directeur général du service juridique de la Commission, Monsieur Ehlermann, qui avait écrit que l'élaboration d'un catalogue propre *sans* adhésion préalable à la CEDH serait perçue comme «une sorte de motion de censure» à l'encontre de cette Convention.[7]

4. Au printemps de 1994, le Parlement a discuté le rapport de la Commission institutionnelle (Fernand Herman) sur le projet d'une constitution de l'Union Européenne sans l'adopter pour autant.[8] C'était la troisième tentative du Parlement en matière constitutionnelle depuis le fameux rapport *Spinelli* de 1984. Dans le catalogue des droits de l'homme de la constitution proposée pour l'Union Européenne l'article 4 sous le titre «liberté de pensée» se lit comme suite:

«*Le droit de la liberté de pensée, conscience et religion est garanti.*»

Après certaines discussions avec des membres du parlement il me semble évident qu'au sein des différents groupes parlementaires il n'existe pas de consensus pour accepter l'article 9 de la CEDH comme base indispensable à la liberté religieuse dans une éventuelle constitution de l'Union.

Jusqu'aujourd'hui le Parlement n'a pas repris le projet de constitution dans son débat en vue de la conférence intergouvernementale en 1996 (Maastricht II).

---

[7] Rapport Bontempi, p. 9.
[8] Rapport de la Commission institutionnelle du Parlement Européen (Hermann) A3-0064/94 du 9.2.1994.

La Commission institutionnelle prépare pour le moment des rapports qui concernent à priori les compétences et les pouvoirs du Parlement vis-à-vis des autres organes de l'Union. En outre, dans le projet de rapport de la Commission institutionnelle du 16 mars 1995[9], une obligation plus évidente de la part de l'Union Européenne à respecter les droits fondamentaux de toutes personnes résidantes dans l'Union Européenne est revendiquée.

Il semble plus réaliste d'enrichir les traités existants d'un catalogue de droits fondamentaux. Cette alternative a été avancée quelque fois dans la littérature et dans la discussion politique. A l'occasion d'un débat international sur l'avenir de l'ordre constitutionnel de l'Union Européenne tenu le 3 mai 1994 à Bonn, Madame le Ministre allemand de la Justice Leutheusser-Schnarrenberger a déclaré avec fermeté qu'un tel catalogue repris dans les traités devrait se situer au niveau de la constitution allemande (Grundgesetz). Cette demande nécessite un débat approfondi avec les autres traditions constitutionnelles.

Il dépendra des discussions entre les églises, de la détermination politique et des résultats des négociations des Etats membres avec les organes de la Communauté si et dans quelle mesure un catalogue de droits fondamentaux pourra être adopté et incorporé dans les traités existants.

II. L'approche concordataire

Le volume de l'activité législative de la Communauté Européenne fait plutôt penser à une relation concordataire au niveau de l'Union Européenne.

Bien que la Commission et le Parlement sont attachés à la neutralité à l'encontre de toute conviction religieuse, philosophique ou idéologique, il faut constater que certains actes législatifs consacrés au fonctionnement du marché intérieur ont des répercussions sur l'autonomie des églises, même sans probablement en avoir l'intention.

Il n'existe pas encore une obligation pour l'Union Européenne de respecter les églises ou les communautés religieuses en tant que telles, de les consulter ou de les faire participer aux diverses commissions, auditions, forums etc.

Comment réaliser une approche concordataire?

[9] Projet d'un rapport de la Commission institutionnelle du Parlement Européen (Martin) du 16.3.1995.

1. Aux termes de l'article 228, la Communauté peut conclure des conventions etc. avec des états ou des organisations internationales. Cet article implique uniquement la compétence institutionnelle; la compétence de la Communauté en droit international se base sur l'article 210.[10]

A priori, l'article 228 n'est pas applicable vu la situation différente de l'église catholique et des églises protestantes.[11] La doctrine considère les concordats du Saint-Siège avec des états comme des accords de droit international, parce que les signataires eux-mêmes sont des personnes juridiques en droit international.

Une opinion contraire, qui gagne actuellement du terrain, affirme que la substance des accords entre l'église et l'état ne relève pas du droit international public au même titre que les intérêts commerciaux, securitaires ou de la circulation.[12]

Les accords entre l'église et l'état règlent plutôt des questions dans le domaine de la société. Il leur manquerait donc une conformité entre le contenu et la forme.

Plusieurs autres éléments, par exemple la nécessité d'une personnalité morale et une certaine séparation entre l'état et les églises rendent également une application analogue difficile à réaliser.

Selon la doctrine des *implied-powers* les compétences explicites du traité peuvent être élargies à l'article 235 à condition qu'une telle mesure s'avère nécessaire afin de réaliser les objectifs de la Communauté. Par conséquent, l'article 235 permet la conclusion de traités internationaux sur base d'une décision unanime du Conseil des Ministres.[13]

2. A part le problème de la compétence de conclure un concordat ou un accord par exemple sur la base des articles 228 ou 235, il convient d'examiner si un objectif de la Communauté pourrait fournir une compétence matérielle pour un tel engagement de sa part. Suite au principe de la subsidiarité (article 3b, paragraphe 1), elle ne peut agir que dans les limites des traités.

> *«La Communauté agit dans les limites des compétences qui lui sont conférées et des objectifs qui lui sont assignés par le présent traité.»*

---

[10] Grabitz-Vedder, *Kommentar zum EWG-Vertrag*, art. 228, Rdw. 3.

[11] Robbers, *Handbuch des Staatskirchenrechts in der Bundesrepublik Deutschland*, p. 331; Turowski, "Staatskirchenrecht der Europäischen Union?", *Kirche und Recht*, 1/95, chiffre 140, p. 4.

[12] Albrecht, *Koordination von Staat und Kirche in der Demokratie*, Freiburg 1965, p. 25-37.

[13] Krück, *Völkerrechtliche Verträge*, p. 93.

Selon le traité la Communauté n'a pas de compétence en matière de cultes ou de religion. Le traité ne lui autorise qu'à fournir «une contribution à l'épanouissement des cultures des Etats membres» (cfr. l'article 3 p et l'article 128) en encourageant la coopération entre les Etats membres dans des domaines limités.

Seul l'article 235 pourrait l'habiliter à conclure un accord avec les églises, si un tel accord était nécessaire pour réaliser les objectifs de la Communauté.

Cet article accorde en effet une compétence générale pour des actes législatifs dans le cadre du marché commun.

La législation de la Cour Européenne a successivement élargi l'application de cet article et permet presque tout acte qui n'empêche pas la réalisation des objectifs du marché commun.

Les relations de la Communauté avec les églises peuvent toucher à des domaines du marché commun, comme la politique sociale, l'enseignement, la formation professionnelle ou la politique de développement. Mais ces points de contact peuvent trouver une solution dans le contexte d'autres formes de coopération.

A priori, une convention ou un accord qui auraient pour objectif la reconnaissance des communautés réligieuses par la Communauté ne figurent pas parmi les objectifs du Marché Commun et nécessiteraient une base formelle par le biais d'une modification du traité (l'article N).

Pour vérifier si la volonté de s'engager pour un tel acte législatif existe, il faudra d'abord engager des discussions entre les églises et les communautés religieuses et passer ensuite à des négociations avec les Etats membres et les organes de l'Union.

III. L'approche coopératrice

Cette approche me semble appropriée dans tous les domaines où les églises, les communautés religieuses, leurs institutions diaconales ou autres s'engagent dans le domaine public.

Une première étape a été réalisée dans l'acte final du Traité de Maastricht, notamment par la déclaration relative à la coopération avec les associations de solidarité:

> «La conférence souligne l'importance que revêt, dans la poursuite des objectifs de l'article 117 du traité instituant la Communauté européenne, une coopération entre celle-ci et les associations de solidarité et les fondations en tant qu'institutions responsables d'établissement et de services sociaux.»

Sur base de cette déclaration les associations de solidarité ont établi une table ronde afin d'approfondir la coopération. Mais elles estiment la déclaration ni suffisante ni assez efficace pour qu'elle puisse former la base d'une coopération permanente et substantielle avec les institutions dans le domaine de la politique sociale européenne. Elles ont pour objectif de faire entrer la coopération avec les associations dans le cadre de l'article 117 dans le traité-même, à l'occasion de la conférence intergouvernementale.

L'intérêt des églises et des communautés religieuses ne se limite pas à la seule coopération. Il s'agit en grande partie aussi de la reconnaissance de leur spécificité et de leur importance pour l'héritage culturel, plus que de leurs relations légales avec les Etats membres dans l'Union Européenne. Ces relations légales ne sont pas suffisamment prises en considération par les institutions européennes, notamment en ce qui concerne la législation.

Actuellement la Commission Européenne essaie de garder une neutralité envers les différentes dénominations religieuses et les différentes religions. Les églises et les communautés doivent veiller à ce que cette neutralité n'empêche pas la coopération mutuelle nonobstant la reconnaissance des spécificités des églises dans la société européenne d'aujourd'hui.

Des implications du droit européen dans les activités des églises et de leurs organisations d'une part et du manque de relations établies entre les églises et l'Union Européenne d'autre part, il ressort une nécessité d'envisager un article en faveur des communautés religieuses dans le traité.

Un tel article peut souligner les objectifs suivants:

– engager les églises et les communautés religieuses dans le processus de la construction européenne,
– obliger l'Union de respecter la diversité des systèmes régissant les relations églises-état au niveau des Etats membres,
– maintenir les compétences pour régler les relations églises-état au niveau des Etats membres,
– protéger contre le refoulement ou le nivellement entre les différents systèmes,
– protéger contre toute forme de discrimination des religions et des communautés religieuses par rapport aux autres organisations dans la société civile,
– créer une base pour des structures appropriées à l'instar des relations églises-état au niveau du droit communautaire.

Probablement la conférence intergouvernementale de 1996 est le moment propice pour entamer le débat sur l'incorporation d'un tel article dans le traité sur l'Union Européenne.

TOWARDS AN INSTITUTIONAL RELATIONSHIP BETWEEN CHURCHES AND THE EUROPEAN UNION

Sophie C. VAN BIJSTERVELD

1. Introduction

The European Union, as we now know it, is a far cry from the Treaty of 1951 which established the European Coal and Steel Community. Through fortunate, and notwithstanding less fortunate, proposals, it is slowly being modelled into a structure that can be defined in terms of a state. The initial Community was paralleled by others, Euratom and the Economic Community. These structures have to a degree been united, their institutions further developed and their powers expanded. The Maastricht Treaty, though revolutionary in its kind, is not the final step. The Treaty itself opens up the future prospect of an evercloser union between the peoples of Europe and designates various stages in this process. However utopian it seemed at the time, the ideal of a United States of Europe as envisioned by Churchill[1] is slowly becoming a reality.

Religion and the church have not been at the heart of developments — they were not expected to be by the European authorities and did not set about achieving this themselves. Along the way churches, however, gradually have taken steps to study and monitor European developments and actions. This is primarily true with regard to the field of social policy.[2] The expansion of the powers and activities of the European institutions and the further development of the institutional framework has given the question of the relationship between churches and the EU a great deal of significance and various options for structuring relationships between the churches and the EU are being proposed and developed.

At present, there are several ideas about how the relationships between the EU and the churches can be structured. First, there are

---

[1] See E. Wistrich, *The United States of Europe*, London/New York 1994, p.26.
[2] Alexander Hollerbach, Europa und das Staatskirchenrecht, in: *Zeitschrift für Evangelisches Kirchenrecht* (35) 1990, p.250-283. Karel Blei, *Kerk-zijn over grenzen heen. Visie op Europa 1992*, Zoetermeer 1992.

church concordats, a familiar construction in various countries of the EU. There are also arrangements with regard to specific areas of church and state relationships such as education, social, and charity work. Thirdly, the relations between church and EU may be shaped through fundamental rights.

In this essay, the relationship between church and EU will be dealt with from the perspective of the fundamental rights approach (without excluding the other options[3]). On the one hand, analysis will show the present deficiency of the fundamental rights approach. On the other hand, this approach may provide the starting point for dealing with the institutional aspects of church and state relationships within the constitutional framework of the EU. Complementary support for defining the future relationship between churches and the EU will be sought in the Treaty system itself.

2. The guarantee of religious freedom in the context of the European Union

In the EC Treaty — which is our main concern — religion as a concept is absent. In the process of expanding EC powers, articles other than those concerning economic powers, such as articles on social policy and education, have found their way into the Treaty.[4] Prior to the codification of these paragraphs, it was clear that national law and policy in areas such as these were affected by spillover effects of EC activities. The awareness of such effects is demonstrated by the insertion of the culture paragraph of Article 128 which in itself stands out as one of the provisions least induced by the economic aims of the Community. Religion, in the framework of the Treaties, is not incorporated as such.

Nevertheless, freedom of religion is part and parcel of Community law. After a cautious start, the Court of Justice applied fundamental rights as part of the "common constitutional tradition of the Member States"[5] the institutions have to abide by. In later rulings, the Court

---

[3] See the contribution of Heidrun Tempel in this volume.

[4] See Articles 126-129A EC Treaty; the EEC already previously had explicit powers with respect to vocational training (Article 127 EEC). The Single European Act introduced competences in the fields of social law and the protection of the environment; see also below par.3.

[5] CJ EG (11/70) 17 December 1970, [1970] ECR 1134 (Internationale Handelsgesellschaft).

made explicit reference to the European Convention on Human Rights.[6] Freedom of religion as guaranteed by Article 9 of the European Convention, therefore, is a principle of law which is of direct relevance to EC law-making.

A confirmation of the significance of the European Convention is given by the Treaty of the Union. Article F expressly states that the Union respects the fundamental rights as guaranteed by the European Convention and as they result from the constitutional traditions common to the Member States. Article L may deny the Court of Justice competence with respect to Article F; its formulation is, in fact, derived from the jurisprudence of the Court.

A closer inspection of freedom of religion as guaranteed in Article 9 of the European Convention shows that its focus is primarily the freedom of religion of the individual.[7] Although it recognizes that an essential element of freedom of religion is the freedom to exercise religion in community with others, Article 9 of the European Convention falls short of dealing with religious communities. Like the Universal Declaration on Human Rights of 1948, the International Covenant on Civil and Political Rights of 1966, the European Convention focuses in Article 9 on the individual person.

Another characteristic of Article 9 of the European Convention is its stress on traditional worship. By way of example, Article 9 mentions various forms of the exercise of religion which are protected. Though the enumeration is clearly not limiting, it is very much concerned with the classic, cultic manifestation of religion. The element which stands out as the most general in its formulation is that of the right to "manifest his religion or belief, in (...) practice and observance".

These two characteristics, the individual focus and the stress upon traditional worship stand out in the rulings of the European Commission on fundamental rights. The somewhat problematic position of the church

---

[6] In CJ EG (4/73) 14 May 1974, [1974] ECR 507 (Nold-II), the Court implicitly referred to the ECHR in its formulation "(i)nternational treaties for the protection of human rights on which the Member States have collaborated or of which they are signatories" which could "supply guidelines" for the Court's ruling; explicit reference to and interpretation of (specific Articles of) the ECHR in later rulings such as CJ 29 October 1980, [1980] ECR 3248 (Van Landewijck). See on this development Henry G. Schermers, Denis Waelbroeck, *Judicial Protection in the European Communities*, Deventer 1992, p.37 ff.

[7] On Article 9 ECHR, Th.C. van Boven, *De volkenrechtelijke bescherming van de godsdienstvrijheid*, Assen 1967. Recently, Jean Duffar, La liberté religieuse dans les textes internationaux, in: *Revue du Droit Public et de la Science Politique en France et a l'Etranger* 1994, p.939-967.

under Article 9 has manifested itself in the rulings of the European Commission concerning the right of appeal under Article 9.[8] It took the European Commission till 1976 to recognize that churches themselves were
protected under Article 9 ECHR following a case of a disciplinary action
against a Danish church minister.[9] After initial denials, the right of
appeal for religious bodies was accepted in 1979. The Commission considered the distinction between churches and their members an artificial
one and stated that when filing a complaint, churches in fact do so as
representatives of their members.[10] With these decisions, the Commission took an important step. The use of the construction of representa-
tion, however, in itself seems artificial and has been justly criticized.[11]
As to the second characteristic, the European Commission, has also
tended to link this guarantee to the manifest ways religion can be exer-
cised. Indirect regulations, i.e., "neutral" regulations, which affect religion or the church as a side-effect were not regarded as falling under the
protection of Article 9.[12]

The interpretation of Article 9 of the Convention which has developed, focusing as it does on the individual and cultic approach, may not
be necessary or satisfactory. It is not surprising either. Church and state
arrangements are very much constructions of national constitutional law.
Worldwide, but also within Europe, various national systems of church
and state relationships exist. Although certain prototypes can be discerned, each is very much determined by its own, often historically
determined, characteristics. The Council of Europe is not concerned with
church and state relationships. Neither is the European Convention.

Within the framework of national church and state systems, the Convention may modify church and state arrangements, but basically leaves
these unaltered. Modifications, as can be expected, are derived from the
perspective of the individual's freedom within the national framework.

The reasoning of the European Commission on Human rights may not
always have been satisfactory. So far major institutional problems have
not occurred as the Council of Europe does not, in fact, engage in spe-

---

[8] Article 25 ECHR which deals with the authority of the European Commission to
handle complaints (see annex) does not in itself mean recognition of protection under
Article 9.

[9] Eur. Comm. H.R. 8 March 1976, App.7374/76, Dec. and Reports 5, 157.

[10] Eur. Comm. H.R. 5 May 1979, App.7805/77, Dec. and Reports 16, 68.

[11] Nikolaus Blum, *Die Gedanken-, Gewissens- und Religionsfreiheit nach Art.9 der
Europäischen Menschenrechtkonvention*, Berlin 1990, p.175.

[12] See Eur. Comm. H.R. 15 December 1983, App.10358/83, Dec. and Reports 37, 142
and Eur. Comm. H.R. 5 July 1984, App.1068/83, Dec. and Reports 39, 267.

cific activities which affect national church and state arrangements. At most, activities have taken place within the Council of Europe which have social of cultural dimensions and stimulate the development and protection of the European heritage.[13] Again, national arrangements of church and state relationships are not directly at stake. As we shall see, this is essentially different with respect to the activities of the EU.

Remarkably, this essential difference with respect to the EU has not yet been given any attention by the drafters of the Constitution of the EU. The draft Constitution of the European Union, which is the annex to a Resolution of the European Parliament[14], guarantees freedom of religion as a fundamental right along with other fundamental rights. Crucially, even more so than in the European Convention, this right is regarded as an individual matter. To stress this, it seems, it is even included under the most conceivable of individualistic rights as "freedom of thought". Article 4, Titel VIII states:

> "Freedom of thought, conscience and religion are guaranteed.
> The right of conscientious objectors to refuse military service shall be guaranteed; the exercise of this right shall not give rise to any discrimination."

Till now, the Court of Justice has seldom had to deal with religion in as direct a manner as the European Commission has. The famous case of Prais, the translator, in which religion and religious freedom was directly at stake, was solved subtly by the Court of Justice without adopting a dogmatic line of reasoning in terms of fundamental rights.[15] The Van Roosmalen Case, concerning the status of a former priest in the context of labour law, was another case which involved religion — and even church and state relationships — but the merit of the case was dealt with as a technical social security law interpretation issue, without referring to religious freedom.[16]

---

[13] A Council of Europe Convention which does fall within the sphere of church-state interests is the Convention of 28 January 1981, concerning the protection of the individual with respect to automated data processing. On another level, initiatives in the field of medical-ethical issues may be a potential area of discussion as well.

[14] Adopted 10 February 1994 (see nt.27).

[15] Case 130/75, *Vivien Prais v. Council of the European Communities* [1976] E.C.R. 1589; [1976] 2 C.M.L.R. 708.

[16] HvJ EG 23 oktober 1986, 300/84, RSV 1987, 94 (*Van Roosmalen v. Bestuur van de Bedrijfsvereniging*). See also G. Robbers, Die Fortentwicklung des Europarechts und seine Auswirkungen auf die Beziehungen zwischen Staat und Kirche in der Bundesrepublik Deutschland, in: *Essener Gespräche* (27) 1993, p.81-100.

These incidental cases must not serve as a disguise for more important and structural issues which may occur. More so than the Prais Case, the Van Roosmalen Case gives the careful reader indications that structural issues may be at stake.

3. A balanced development

Although the basic discussion on the place of religion and belief and the institutional position of the church within the European Union has yet to take place, there are various signs within the constitutional discussion on the European level itself that a balanced constitutional development is essential.[17] The result in terms of Treaty provisions, however, complex,[18] and the overall process of development so far has triggered critical reactions.[19]

Was the Single European Act concerned with the realization of the internal market in 1992 and the introduction of new compentences to be viewed in the perspective of this economic aim, the Maastricht Treaty reaches beyond this aspiration. It is not only the Union itself with the hesitant introduction of the new intergovernmental pillars, its definition of its ends, and the principles reflected in its Considerations[20] that gives evidence of this. The transformation of the EEC Treaty into the EC Treaty[21] is as significant.

It has been pointed out that the latter transformation is double-edged. On the one hand, the adoption of the new competences in the field of education, culture, public health, and consumer protection are the result of the understanding that economic reality must not take precedence over other areas of life. On the other hand, these competences are unmistakably limited; the formulation of each of these new articles is — to a varying degree — imbued with the idea of subsidiarity which in general wordings is codified in the new Article 3B.[22] As these policy areas were

[17] See also the contribution of Gerhard Robbers in this volume.

[18] See T. Koopmans, Europe and its lawyers in 1984, CMLRev. 1985, p.9-18.

[19] See D.M. Curtin, The Constitutional Structure of the Union: a Europe of Bits and Pieces, in: K. Hellingman (red.), Europa in de Steigers: van Gemeenschap tot Unie, Deventer 1993, p.1 ff.

[20] See notably the Considerations (1), (2), (3) (6) and (12).

[21] Dropping the "Economic" character of the Community and, in connection with this the redefinition of its aims and the adoption of the new competences under express adherence to the principle of subsidiarity.

[22] P.J.G. Kapteyn, De Complexe Rechtsorde van het Unieverdrag: subsidiariteitsbeginsel en nieuwe bevoegdheden, in: K. Hellingman (red.), Europa in de Steigers: van Gemeenschap tot Unie, Deventer 1993, p.41 ff.

influenced by EC activities prior to the alteration of the E(E)C Treaty, their legal significance is primarily to control EC activities in these areas so that (side-)effects are taken into account and a basis for "national interest" exemptions in these fields is provided.[23]

The implication of this for our topic is two-fold. The general adhesion to the principle of subsidiarity and proportionality, as well as the specified formulation of these principles in the context of the "new competences", clearly limit EC activity and provide a framework for vertical power dispersion. Fundamental rights, as adhered to by the Court of Justice, of course, further require power limitation.[24] These circumstances analogously point towards a reserve when it comes down to religion.

The idea behind adoption of the "new competences" and the extension of the scope of the EC Treaty, which give evidence of the need of an understanding of society which goes beyond the principles of economics, have relevance in this respect as well. To this may be added the Considerations preceding the provisions of the Treaty of Maastricht.[25] These observations are in line with the opinion that sensitivity to the value of religion in this context is needed.[26]

Similar ideas can be discerned in the draft of a Constitution of the European Union[27]. The explanatory memorandum to the draft justifies the need for a Constitution in political,[28] legal (juridical),[29] and ethical terms. In each of these areas, the non-material basis of the Union stands out.

In general terms, these signs lead to the conclusion that there is a striving for a balanced development of a (European) society, which is open to the material interests and the material welfare of the individuals and nations. At the same time, sound development requires a sense of the moral dimension of society, the social coherence of society, and the need to keep alive the questions of the transcendency of human life.

---

[23] P.J.G. Kapteyn (nt.22), p.52.

[24] Starting point is Article 4 EC-Treaty.

[25] See notably the Conderations (1), (2), (3), (6) and (12).

[26] We may also point at Article 118B EC Treaty, which in referring to the Social Partners, recognizes the social reality of intermediate bodies. In doing so, the Treaty reaches beyond a mere "frame of government" and specification of the position of the private individual.

[27] Doc.-En\RR\244\244403, PE 203.601/fin; A3-0031/94.

[28] The memorandum speaks of "an axis of stability" which must be formed. Its "size and material power, and also its moral strength" should set an example to the new democracies of the East (p.22).

[29] Reference is made to acknowledgement by the Court of Justice that the Community contains a constitutional legal order, certain aspects of which cannot be put under discussion, not even through Treaty revision (p.22).

The importance of non-material welfare and, at the same time, the somewhat ambivalent position of public authority with respect to value questions[30] account for the fact that the church — traditionally one of the main, if not the main, articulators in this field — distinguishes itself from organizations and that church and state arrangements form basic principles of the national constitutional order.

4. The impact of Community law on national church and state law

The very fact that church and state arrangements form basic principles of the national constitutional order requires that the EU respect them. At first sight, it may seem that the European institutions do not infringe on these arrangements. Speaking of direct infringements, this is probably true. Infringements can, however, be indirect. Often the infringements may be a side-effect of measures which are not pertinent to religion at all.

When we take a closer look at national church-state law, we see that it covers a wide range. National church and state legal studies are concerned with areas ranging from tax law to labour law, from data protection law to mass media law. From this it is clear that EC law influences national church and state law. In each of these areas, respect for national arrangements is required. It is also clear that these fields involve structural arrangements beyond the individual perspective of religious freedom.

EC institutions increasingly conduct activities in areas of law that affect the position of church and religion. Awareness on a European level of the range of issues involved and knowledge of the national church and state systems is therefore first of all required.

The obligation to respect national church and state structures should be expressly mentioned in the Treaty system of the EU. Such an obligation would easily fit into the general framework which already exists. In this context, we may point directly to the principles of subsidiarity and proportionality which are incorporated in the EC Treaty and are referred to in the Maastricht Treaty. These notions find a central place in the draft of a European Constitution as well.

Reference has already been made to the culture paragraph, Article 128, of the EC Treaty. This paragraph gives evidence of the sensitivity to spill-over effects of measures which are not primarily concerned with culture, but nevertheless affect it. An analogous construction may be

---

[30] See C.J. Klop, *De cultuurpolitieke paradox. Noodzaak èn onwenselijkheid van overheidsinvloed op normen en waarden*, Kampen 1993.

thought of with respect to national church and state law, though preferably in a somewhat more compelling formulation.[31]

The European "involvement" with church and religion should not stop with merely respecting national church and state structures. Involvement is needed at a second level as well. EC institutions should, on the one hand, respect the structures of church and state arrangements in the countries of the European Union. On the other hand, the EC (the Union) itself needs to develop an understanding of its relationship to the church.

This could generate a fruitful and open dialogue on issues that are at the core of the values that the EU wishes to foster and could be part and parcel of the further development of a united Europe in which non-material values are taken seriously. A concrete example could be the protection of the collective day of rest within the working hours Directive or the restriction on tv commercials in the television Directive.[32] Again, the considerations in the Maastricht Treaty and draft of the Constitution point in that direction.

How should we picture such a relationship and how should this be legally formulated? A closer look at the concluding document of the Vienna meeting of the CSCE reveals the presence of a quite elaborate paragraph on religion. It is striking that this document — which does not have the status of a binding Treaty — contains elements that give evidence of a certain understanding of the role of religion and religious communities within society and the legal needs which are a consequence thereof.[33]

The document is concerned with the status of religious communities as legal persons within their country, the right to organize themselves freely and to maintain their organization through, among other things, education and appointments, and to relieve their financial needs.[34] The states have the obligation to respect them. In this document, furthermore, two very important elements stand out. These are concerned with opportunities for churches to manifest their role in society within as well as outside their own private sphere.

---

[31] A concrete formulation has been proposed by Gerhard Robbers.

[32] Council Directive 93/104, *OJ EG L 307* of 13 December 1993, p.13; Council Directive 89/552, *OJ EG L 289*, of 3 October 1989, p.23.

[33] The Vienna meeting must also be seen within the specific politcal context of the time.

[34] It is formulated as an obligation of the States and in the perspective of individual freedom, but it exceeds the individual focus by far.

(The States are obliged to ...)

> "16e* engage in consultations with religious faiths, institutions and orga-
> nizations in order to achieve a better understanding of the requirements of
> religious freedom; ...
> 16k* favorably consider the interest of religious communities in partici-
> pating in public dialogue, inter alia, through mass media;"[35]

These two types of commitment could function pre-eminently in an
EU which does not yet have a tradition of hundreds of years in commu-
nicating with religions.[36]

5. Summary

International guarantees of religious freedom focus on the individual
rather than on the institutional aspect of religion. Although it is recog-
nized that an essential element of freedom of religion is the freedom to
exercise religion in community with others, treaty provisions fall short
of dealing with religious communities.

EC institutions increasingly engage in activities in areas of law that
affect the position of church and religion. Awareness on a European
level of the range of issues involved is therefore required.

EC institutions should respect the structures of church and state
arrangements in the countries of the European Union. This should be
explicitly formulated in the Treaty structure. This idea easily fits into
the general principles concerning the competence balance between
EU and Member States and the desire for a balanced development of
a European Union demonstrated in the considerations of the Maastricht Treaty. It also has a concrete example in the structure on culture.

On the other hand, the EC (the Union) itself needs to develop an
understanding of its relationship to the church. In this instance too, the
balanced development of a European Union is at stake. Religous freedom goes beyond the notion of individual freedom. A proper and realistic view of the value and functioning of religion in society realizes this.
The Concluding document of the Vienna meeting of the CSCE provides
elements for orientation.

---

[35] Concluding Document Vienna Meeting CSCE (17 January 1989), contained in
International Legal Materials (28) 1989, nr.1, p.531 ff. (p.534).

[36] Also other intermediate bodies feature in the Treaty; social partners are granted a
position in the policy making process.

Without excluding other options, such as concordats or specific arrangements on certain subjects, adoption of an appropriate provision in the Treaty structure of the Union should be the future prospective. Church and state arrangements are part of the basic national constitutional order, to the extent they are visible in the very document that lies at the basis of and structures that constitutional order. This should not be different in a European constitutional order.

* The author acknowledges with gratitude the comments and suggestions of Drs. Mark Vitullo with regard to the translation of the manuscript.

Annex

Article 9 ECHR:

"1. Everyone has the right to freedom of thought, conscience and religion; this right includes freedom to change his religion or belief and freedom, either alone or in community with others and in public or private, to manifest his religion or belief, in worship, teaching, practice and observance.
2. Freedom to manifest one's religion or beliefs shall be subject only to such limitations as are prescribed by law and are necessary in a democratic society in the interests of public safety, for the protection of public order, health or morals, or for the protection of the rights and freedoms of others."

Article 25 ECHR:

"1. The Commission may recive petitions addressed to the Secretary General of the Council of Europe from any person, non-governmental organisation or group of individuals claiming to be the victim of a violation by one of the High Contracting Parties of the rights set forth in this Convention, provided that the High Contracting Party against which the complaint has been lodged has declared that it recognises the competence of the Commission to receive such petitions. Those of the High Contracting Parties who have made such a declaration undertake not to hinder in any way the effective exercise of this right.
(....)"

Article 3B EC Treaty:

"The Community shall act within the limits of the powers conferred upon it by this Treaty and of the objectives assinged to it therein.
In areas which do not fall within its exclusive comptence, the Community shall take action, in accordance with the principle of subsidiarity, only if and in so far as the objectives of the proposed action cannot be sufficiently achieved by the Member States and can therefore, by reason of the scale or effects of the proposed action, be better achieved by the Community.
Any action by the Community shall not go beyond what is necessary to achieve the objectives of this Treaty."

Article 118B EC Treaty:

"The Commission shall endeavour to develop the dialogue between management and labour at European level which could, if the two sides consider it desirable, lead to relations based on agreement."

Article 128 EC Treaty:

"1. The Community shall contribute to the flowering of the cultures of the Member States, while respecting their national and regional diversity and at the same time bringing the common cultural heritage to the fore.

2. Action by the Community shall be aimed at encouraging cooperation between Member States and, if necessary, supporting and supplementing their action in the following areas:
- improvement of the knowledge and dissemination of the culture and history of the European peoples;
- conservation and safeguarding of cultural heritage of European significance;
- non-commercial cultural exchanges;
- artistic and literary creations, including in the audiovisual sector.

3. The Community and the Member States shall foster cooperation with third countries and the competent international organizations in the sphere of culture, in particular the Council of Europe.

4. The Community shall take cultural aspects into account in its action under other provisions of this Treaty.

5. In order to contribute to the achievement of the objectives referred to in this Article, the Council:
- acting in accordance with the procedure referred to in Article 189b and after consulting the Committee of the Regions, shall adopt incentive measures, excluding any harmonization of the laws and regulations of the Member States. The Council shall act unanimously throughout the procedures referred to in Article 189b;
- acting unanimously on a proposal from the Commission, shall adopt recommendations."

CHURCH AND STATE IN EUROPE.
COMMON PATTERN AND CHALLENGES

Silvio Ferrari

1. The aim of my paper is to illustrate (a) that there is a common pattern of Church-State relations in the member states of the European Union and (b) that this pattern could provide some help in defining a common European legal framework encompassing the national Church-State systems. The challenges to the common pattern which arise from the changes that have recently occurred in the religious landscape of Western Europe will be discussed in the final part of the paper.

The discussion will provide just a rough outline of the question. I would like to single out the main features of the existing national legal systems and in a second step examine the possibilities these open up for defining some common principles at European level. The purpose is to indicate a possible way of dealing with Church-State problems in the framework of the European Union. There can be no doubt however that such a way will still need to be tested through a much more detailed analysis.

2. The traditional classification of Church - State systems in Western Europe is based on a tripartition: separation systems, concordatarian systems and national Church systems.

This classification is outdated and of little use in understanding what is going on in the field of Church - State relations. It over-emphasises the formal side of these relationships and does not pay enough attention to their content. Therefore it is of little use in identifying whether a common model is taking shape, even though the means used to make it may be very different. Of course, I am not saying it is the same to discipline Church-State relations through a concordat or through a State law[1]. According to many scholars, provisions contained in a concordat have the same strength as provisions of international law and cannot be modified unilaterally. They therefore award stronger protection to the

---

[1] The topic is discussed by J. Martinez-Torrón, *Separatismo y cooperación en los acuerdos del Estado con las minorías religiosas* (Granada: Comares, 1994).

Churches than State laws. But the signing of a concordat does not seem to be the qualifying element of the State's attitude toward a Church, neither from a political nor from a legal point of view. There is no concordat In Belgium, yet the Catholic Church enjoys a better legal position there than in some countries where a concordat has been stipulated.

Much of what has been said may also be applied to the legal status of the Churches in the State. In Germany and Greece, for instance, the Churches enjoy the status of public law, while in The Netherlands and in France they have a status of private law. Again, the public law/private law status is not the decisive factor if we approach the question of Church-State relations from the point of view of their content[2]. In Ireland Churches are not corporations of public law, but their legal position is as strong as that of the German Churches which are public law corporations.

3. At this point I think it is possible to detect a common pattern of Church-State relations in Western Europe, although this pattern is applied in different ways.

These are the main features of the pattern:

a) At the individual level there is the neutral (impartial) attitude of the State toward the various religious subjects who are free to profess the religion they prefer.

b) At the collective level there is the outline, inside the "public" sector, of a ~religious~ sub-sector (or domain or playing field or protected area)[3] where the different religious subjects can enjoy preferential treatment compared to non-religious subjects.

c) At both levels the State's right to interfere with religious subjects is confined to making the rules of the game and seeing to it that the boundaries of the domain are respected.

The same pattern can be detected in the structure of the international and constitutional legal provisions concerning religious freedom and Church-State relations in Western Europe[4].

---

[2] See H.J. Kiderlen, in Die *Einigung Europas und die Staat-Kirche-Ordnung (Essener Gespräche zum Thema Staat und Kirche, 27)* (Münster: Aschendorff, 1993) 104.

[3] About the notion of "protected area" see P. Batelaan, "L'école dans une société multireligieuse", in Conseil de l'Europe (ed.), *Liberté de conscience* (Strasbourg: Conseil de l'Europe, 1993) 181.

[4] See J. Duffar, "Le régime constitutionnel des cultes", in European Consortium for Church-State Research, *The Constitutional Position of the Churches in Europe. Proceedings of the meeting of Paris*, November 18-19, 1994 (Paris-Milano: Litec-Giuffrè, 1995)

These provisions call for an impartial attitude of the public authorities. The latter are bound to respect the right to profess any religion (art. 9, first paragraph of the European Convention on Human Rights (ECHR); most Western European constitutions contain similar provisions) and to avoid discriminations based on religion (art. 14 of the ECHR; art. 3 of the Italian Constitution; art. 2 of the French Constitution; art. 14 of the Spanish Constitution, etc.). They protect the internal autonomy of religious denominations to an extent which is not guaranteed to non-religious associations (art. 8 of the Italian Constitution; art. 137 of the Weimar Constitution incorporated in the German Constitution; art. 44 of the Irish Constitution, etc.) and contain favourable provisions for the denominations' external activities such as the teaching of religion in State schools, religious assistance in the Army, the building of places of worship and so on (art. 7 of the German Constitution; art. 127 of the Belgian Constitution, etc. Similar provisions are more often to be found in non-constitutional laws)[5]. These provisions outline the playing field where religious subjects enjoy preferential treatment. Finally a limit (such as morals, public order, health, safety, third party rights) to the expression of religious freedom is always included (art. 9, second paragraph of the ECHR; art. 8 and 19 of the Italian Constitution; art. 5 of the Greek Constitution, etc.), to mark the rules of the game and the boundaries of the playing field.

Of course this picture simplifies the complexity and the nuances presented by the different legal systems.

First of all a careful task of definition would be necessary as some words have different meanings in different countries. The internal autonomy of the religious community, for example, has a much wider content in Germany, where it also covers the educational and social activities of the Churches than in Spain, where it covers just the religious activities. This means that to grant the internal autonomy of the religious communities as a feature of the European pattern would have a different impact on European labour law, trade union law and competition law according to the meaning of the word "autonomy".

Secondly, while the pattern is the same almost everywhere in Western Europe, its practical translations vary from country to country.

(in press); J. van der Vyver, "Legal Dimension of Religious Human Rights. Constitutional Texts", in *Religious Human Rights in the World Today. Proceedings of the meeting of Atlanta, October 6-9, 1994* (in press).

[5] See for example European Consortium for Church-State Research (ed.), *Church and State in Europe. State Financial Support. Religion and the School* (Milano: Giuffrè, 1992); Id., Marriage and Religion in Europe (Milano: Giuffrè, 1993).

For example, if we consider the teaching of religion in State schools, it is easy to find a difference between France, where no teaching is provided, and Italy, where the teaching of one (or more) religions is guaranteed. However, this difference appears to depict a different degree of cooperation between the public powers and the religious institutions rather than a lack of cooperation. Even in France (which is "le seul Etat laïc d'Europe" according to its then Minister of the Interior, Mr. Pasqua)[6] chaplains have access to secondary schools and the primary school timetable is arranged in such a way as to allow students to have a religious education without any hindrance.

The same happens in the field of religious assistance, which is provided in French prisons, hospitals and the Army by chaplains paid by the State. It can be found to a lesser degree even in the field of financing, as Churches enjoy some tax exemptions and donations (in favour of religious communities) which can be deducted from the taxes the donors have to pay.

Of course it is possible to say that the system of religious teaching or religious assistance which exist in Italy or Germany is more favourable to the Churches than the French one. But it would be wrong to say that the French State does not cooperate at all with the Churches in these areas. In other words, there are different versions of a common model, rather than an alternative model. Following the classification of Church-State systems recently proposed by Cole Durham[7] we may conclude that the models prevailing in the member States of the European Union range from benevolent separation to cooperation, i.e. within quite narrow limits.

At the same time we should also recognise that there are some features of national laws which are not a particular version of the pattern but indeed contradict the pattern itself. That is the case, for example, of the prohibition of proselytism in Greece (art. 13, par. 2 of the Greek Constitution; see also the case Greece v. Kokkinakis decided by the European Court of Human Rights)[8] and, in my opinion, also of the prohibition of a religious marriage without a previous civil marriage in France, Germany and Belgium.

---

[6] Inauguration de la Mosquee de Lyon. Allocution de Monsieur Charles Pasqua, le 30 septembre 1994.

[7] W. Cole Durham, "A Comparative Framework for Analyzing Religious Liberty", in *Religious Human Rights in the World Today* (in press).

[8] Eur. Court H.R., Kokkinakis v. Greece judgement of 25 May 1993, Series A no. 260-A.

4. With regard to the European law, the relationship between the common pattern on the one hand and the different national systems on the other could be defined as a relationship between the "common constitutional tradition" of the members of the European Union and the "national identities" of the same members recalled in art. F of the Treaty on the European Union.

The first (the common pattern constituting the "common constitutional tradition") is at the core of the European Union identity from the point of view of Church-State relations. Taking this as the starting point it is possible to work out some legal provisions containing the principles underlying the attitude of the European Union attitude towards religion and the religious communities. The first and the third features of the pattern (as defined under letters a) and c) in paragraph 3 of this paper) are already included in European Union law through the reference which is made in art. F of the European Union Treaty to art. 9 of the ECHR in which the protection of religious freedom and the limits to its manifestation are set out. Therefore the remaining work would be confined to bringing the second feature of the pattern (letter b, paragraph 3) into the European legal system. This is the feature concerning the internal autonomy of the religious communities and State cooperation with some of their external activities.

The various national systems can be seen as a part of the national identities. These should be respected as essential components of the common European heritage, as far as they do not conflict with the features of the common pattern. In other words, national provisions conflicting with the common pattern are not protected under art. F of the Treaty of the European Union. This area should be reserved to national laws, which will provide the concrete legal provisions which govern Church-State relations in each country.

In order to give expression to such a relationship in the European legal order a provision could be conceived where, on the one hand, the three features of the common pattern are confirmed and, on the other, a general reservation clause is included, which prevents the European Union from invading the field reserved to national competence. The reservation clause would be an application of the subsidiarity principle embodied in art. 3 of the European Community Treaty[9]. Deciding which

---

[9] See G. Robbers, "Die Fortentwicklung des Europarechts und seine Auswirkungen auf die Beziehungen zwischen Staat und Kirche in der Bundesrepublik Deutschland" in *Die Einigung Europas und die Staat-Kirche Ordnung (Essener Gespräche zum Thema Staat und Kirche, 27)* (Münster: Aschendorff, 1993), 85-86.

is the best system of religious teaching or religious financing in Italy has to be left to Italy because that system is strictly related to Italian history, culture, tradition, etc.

This conclusion also provides some guidelines for dealing with the challenges arising from recent developments in the field of Church-State relations. While the main features of the pattern have to be safeguarded, the different Church-State systems exist in the EU countries also provide more room for experiment, in which new solutions can be tested.

7. From the point of view of the Christian Churches, the pattern does not appear to present any insurmountable difficulties.

Apart from the fact that one root of the pattern can be traced to the Christian distinction between God and Caesar (while a second root goes back to the Enlightenment), the pattern itself has not recently come up against criticism from Church authorities, with the exception of some minority groups, particularly among Catholics. Indeed the pattern seems to have provided a good framework for bridging the gap between the modern world and the Churches. This gap was still very wide a century ago, at least in Catholic countries.

Of course there are some sensitive areas, particularly where the internal autonomy of the Churches conflicts with the fundamental rights of individuals. The labour law inside Churches and religious organisations is a good example of such a conflict[10]. Another delicate point is when the freedom of religion conflicts with other equally important liberties such as freedom of speech. But the solutions provided by national and international courts and in particular by the Commission and the Court on Human Rights (see the recent decision in the case Austria v. Otto Preminger Institut)[11] have always been carefully balanced. It has thus been possible to tackle these issues within a good theoretical framework, which could be further improved through a better knowledge of US jurisprudence on "compelling State interest" and the "least restrictive alternative".

This conclusion does not mean there are no problems left to be dealt with. One major objection to the common European pattern is that it does not include among its features an equal treatment of the religious communities. But this is because equal treatment is lacking first of all in

---

[10] See European Consortium for Church-State Research (ed.), *Churches and Labour Law in the EC Countries* (Milano-Madrid: Giuffrè-Facultad de Derecho, 1993).
[11] European Court of Human Rights, September 20, 1994 (11/1993/406/48).

national laws, which are inclined to give better opportunities to older, larger and "mainstream" religious communities[12]. As this is the situation in the member States, it is difficult, indeed almost impossible, for the European Union to set a standard that differs radically from those which exist in the national legislation.

A second problem might arise if the expansion of the EU toward the East brings more Orthodox Churches into the Union. The Orthodox system of Church-State relations is based on an all-encompassing notion of religion, where the latter is considered the synthesis of the history and the culture of a nation. By consequence, the Orthodox system is consequently inclined to view the dominant Church as a national institution and the remaining religious communities as "foreign" denominations. The upshot is that religion gains a pervasive influence over the entire public sector and therefore beyond the borders of the sub-sector assigned to it (i.e. to religion). What is more, disparities in the legal treatment of the various religious communities become accentuated beyond the limits imposed by the principle of impartiality of the public powers. But such an enlargement of the EU does not seem to be near at hand and the Church-State systems in Eastern Europe are changing so quickly that it is difficult to assess the final outcome of this process of transformation.

8. The greatest pressure is from outside the Christian world. In the religious landscape of the EU two important changes have taken place in the last 20 years: the spread of the Islam as well as of the "new" religious movements.

Islam is challenging the pattern because it does not consider religion to be a sub-sector inside a larger playing field. For Islam religion is the playing field itself where every other subject (economic, political, cultural, etc.) has to play: it is no coincidence that in Arabic the same word — "umma" — defines religious society and political society.

---

[12] It has been said "a multi-tiered structure of religious entities [...] is characteristic of many European countries, and so long as such a scheme is administered fairly in ways that minimize distinctive burdens for religious minorities and that do not inhibit the practice of minority religions" there is no violation of international human rights norms requiring equal treatment (W. Cole Durham, Jr., *Analysis of Pending Lithuanian Legislation on Religious Freedom and Religious Organizations*, typewritten text, January 23, 1995, 14). While consenting with this analysis, it is possible to wonder whether the equal treatment rule is respected when some religious communities enjoy advantages which are denied to others in many and important areas (financing by the State, access to mass media, possibility of teaching religion in State schools, etc.). Moreover the rules governing the allotment of the advantages are different and largely discretionary. It is therefore also difficult to affirm that each religious community gets (if not the same) at least its own.

This point is clear when reading the Islamic declarations on human rights, where it is evident that the ultimate foundation of human rights is not legal but theological. Article 24 of the Cairo Declaration on Human Rights in Islam (1990) affirms that "all the rights and freedoms stipulated in this Declaration are subject to the Islamic Shari'ah"[13]. The law, and therefore also the right to religious freedom, remains subordinate to religion.

This assumption — which makes the legal and social order depending upon the tenets of one religion — cannot be accommodated with the Western European pattern of Church-State relations. It encroaches on its first feature, namely that the freedom to choose, profess and change any religion is a right which belongs to every individual. To yield in this area would be incompatible with the very core of European civilisation.

But that does not mean that the safeguarding of the pattern will necessarily drive us to a clash with Islam: the pattern is flexible enough to make room for Islam without losing its significance and usefulness.

The presence of a large Islamic community in Europe is very likely going to become permanent. This presence will necessarily influence the third feature of the pattern, i.e. the limits to religious freedom. These limits are largely inherited from a period when the Western European culture was mostly Christian, or rather, a mix of Christian and secular values. The notions of public order or public morals were and still are permeated with a Christian background. But in the long run the same notions cannot help undergoing a process of transformation due to the permanent, and numerically increasing, presence of a large community with different backgrounds. Some steps of this process have already been made: some countries recognise — although timidly — the right to abstain from work on Friday afternoon, for example. Other steps are currently under discussion, and sometimes harsh discussion, such as the right to wear religious symbols in schools. Sooner or later, further steps will become the subject of discussion, for instance the right to recognition in Europe of poligamic marriages concluded in countries where poligamy is admitted.

To avoid any misunderstanding, I would like to stress that these arguments do not mean to express any judgment as to the political opportunity of introducing these innovations into the laws of the European countries. They only raise the issue as to whether it is juridically possible to

---

[13] The Declaration text is in G. Martin Muñoz (ed.), *Democracia y derechos humanos en el mundo arabe* (Madrid: ICMA, 1993) 297-317.

continue to reject them on the basis of a notion of public order that for various reasons appears obsolete. I am not even claiming that every religion, or culture, has the same value so that the notions of public order or morals have to undergo an indiscriminate transformation just because a religious, or cultural, community has taken its roots in Europe. European civilisation, as any other civilisation, is based on the recognition of a number of principles which are considered either of universal value — and so affirmed everywhere — or of fundamental significance for the European identity — and so applied to everybody who wants to live permanently in Europe. Such is the case, for example, of the enjoyment of civil and political rights assured to everybody irrespective of his or her religion or conviction, or change of religion. But not everything which currently comes under the notion of public order or morality has to be numbered among these fundamental principles.

A carefully balanced evolution of the concepts of public order and morality may be the easiest way to accommodate Islam within the European pattern of Church-State relations and at the same time to make that pattern acceptable to the Islamic community. This process would greatly contribute to the birth of a European Islam, whose historic role would be to bear witness of the possibility of a composition between Islamic religion and European civilisation. This is, in my opinion, the only lasting solution to the question of Muslim immigration in Europe.

9. The second challenge to the common pattern outlined above comes from the "new" religious movements. Frequently they propose an "all-encompassing" concept of the religious experience, to the extent that they absorb — and according to some, condition — the entire personality of the follower. Some of their adherents are so absorbed in their religious practices and activities that they do not care about the possible dangers that these practices may have on their physical and psychological integrity.

The question has already been dealt with by the European Council which decided, in my opinion correctly, against any special legislative provisions limiting the freedom of the "new" religious movements[14].

---

[14] See Conseil de l'Europe. Assemblée parlementaire. Recommandation 1178/92 relative aux sectes et aux nouveaux mouvements religieux, 5 février 1992; Conseil de l'Europe. Assemblée parlementaire. Communication du Comité des Ministres. Réponse complémentaire à la Recommandation 1178/92 relative aux sectes et aux nouveaux mouvements religieux, 21 février 1994 (these documents are published in *Quaderni di diritto e politica ecclesiastica*, 1993/2, 491-92 and 1994/2, 535-37).

National legal systems already provide instruments to repress eventual abuses and special legislation would have been questionable from the point of view of the right to religious liberty.

But the "new" religious movements also put into question the common pattern albeit from a different angle. They call into question the principle of impartiality, i.e. the first feature of the pattern. They claim that the State in reality uses a selective notion of religion and they point at the scientific weaknesses of the criteria adopted to define the legal notion of religion[15].

The terms of the question are well known. The traditional notion of religion has been obtained from Christianity, Judaism and Islam, in other words from those religions that the European environment has had the most contact with. This notion does not suit other religious experiences such as Buddhism, to mention only one, that have developed in areas which are distant geographically speaking, from the Mediterranean basin. These religions have only recently penetrated Europe with a significant number of followers.

The criticism focuses on the "ideological" use of the legal notion of religion and therefore at the existence of an (unavowed) "access card". This system selects the subjects which are allowed to act in the sub-sector "religion" and enjoy the advantages associated with this membership. Selection is based on the preferences of public opinion and institutions.

This criticism is not unfounded. Up to now the attempts to formulate a legal definition of religion which is sufficiently comprehensive but not so broad as to be useless have not been very successful. Therefore national administrative powers have taken different and frequently discretionary decisions. Even inside the European Union, it may happen that the religious character is awarded to a religious group in one State and denied to the same group in another State[16].

---

[15] See R.O. Frame, "Belief in a Nonmaterial Reality. A Proposed First Amendment Definition of Religion", in *University of Illinois Law Review*, 1992, n. 3, 819-52; A. Motilla, *Sectas y derecho en España* (Madrid: Editoriales de derecho reunidas, 1990); P. Badura, *Der Schutz von Religion und Weltanschauung durch das Grundgesetz* (Tübingen: Mohr, 1989); S. Ferrari (ed.), *Diritti dell'uomo e libertà dei gruppi religiosi. Problemi giuridici dei nuovi movimenti religiosi* (Padova: Cedam, 1989); Id., "La nozione giuridica di confessione religiosa (come sopravvivere senza conoscerla)", *Proceedings of the meeting "Principio pattizio e relatà religiose minoritarie"*. (Urbino, October 22-24, 1993) (in press).

[16] See for example the Proceedings of the meeting of Strasbourg (December 1-2, 1994) on *Les cultes reconnus en Europe*.

The problem could be solved, at least in theory, by enforcing a strict regime of separation between Church and State so that each religious organisation — from the oldest Church to the latest "sect" — would be considered a private association. But this is not a path the European States are going to follow. Therefore the only way out — though it is not a completely satisfactory solution — is an empirical one. On the one hand, when dealing with the question of the religious or non-religious character of a group, it is necessary to bear in mind that the traditional paradigm of religion is wearing thin before the important and rapid changes that are taking place in the world of religious faiths. In such a situation it is important to accept a broad definition of religion, as suggested in the UN Human Rights Committee's interpretation of art. 18, par. 2 of the International Covenant on Civil and Political Rights[17]. On the other side, the legal recognition of the religious nature of a group should be removed from the area of the discretionary powers of the administration and should be brought under the control of the judiciary power, as already happens in some European States.

[17] See Human Rights Committee, General Comment n. 22(48) concerning art. 18 (CCPR/C/21/rev.l/Add.4, 27 September 1993).

LE DROIT APPLIQUE AUX EGLISES ET RELIGIONS EN FRANCE ET EN RFA.

APPROCHE COMPARATIVE DE CERTAINS ELEMENTS

Francis MESSNER

La construction de l'Europe, pour être viable et efficace, doit intégrer tous les aspects de la vie en société y compris les aspects religieux. Les systèmes de relation entre les États et les religions en sont une des composantes.

Ces systèmes, très marqués historiquement, sont hétérogènes et parfois caractérisés par une diversité au sein du territoire national (France: droit général et droits locaux; RFA: le droit des cultes est de la compétence des États fédérés).

Ce pluralisme des statuts cultuels et plus largement du droit appliqué au phénomène religieux ne saurait exclure une réflexion sur l'élaboration d'un statut de base des institutions religieuses et de conception de l'univers dans l'Union Européenne.

Ce statut correspondrait à un plus petit commun dénominateur du droit des religions en Europe. Fondé sur les principes supra-législatifs de liberté de religion, d'égalité en matière religieuse et de neutralité de l'État, il garantirait à l'ensemble des religions et des groupements de conceptions de l'univers un cadre juridique dont les éléments restent à préciser collectivement (constitution en association ou en établissement, droit social et du travail des ministres du culte et des permanents pastoraux, soutien public pour la mise en œuvre de la garantie de liberté de religion, exonérations fiscales, etc.).

Mais pour déboucher sur une solution consensuelle, il convient, d'emblée, de prendre en compte les différences, les points de résistance identitaire souvent masqués sous des concepts communs constituant l'originalité des divers systèmes. C'est en regard de cette perspective que je présenterai certains éléments caractéristiques des droits appliqués aux religions en France et en RFA.

1. La liberté d'organisation des cultes (France) ou des communautés religieuses (RFA)

La liberté d'organisation des Églises et religions, encore appelée liberté institutionnelle constitue un des éléments clés des divers statuts des Églises et religions en Europe. Il convient toutefois de distinguer les formes variées que peut prendre cette liberté avant même d'en déplorer dans certains cas l'absence.

Ainsi, certaines Églises populaires nordiques comme la Suède ont choisi d'être des Églises démocratiques où tout pouvoir émane du peuple dans le cadre des institutions politiques du pays. En ce sens le système hiérarchique catholique romain ne peut pas constituer l'unique référence pour déterminer le contenu de cette liberté.

Différente serait inversement l'hypothèse d'un cadre juridique imposé par l'État, ne prenant en compte aucune facette de cette liberté. Ce cas de figure est quasi inexistant à l'heure actuelle en Europe.

Enfin, l'exemple de la Confédération Helvétique ne manque pas d'originalité dans la mesure où l'État et les forces sociales ont réussi à mettre en œuvre des fonctionnements démocratiques dans l'Église catholique sur la base d'un large consensus, qui n'est pas remis en cause par le Saint-Siège.

Mais la liberté institutionnelle des Églises et religions n'a pas le même contenu selon les pays. Il peut être restreint ou au contraire très étendu.

Ainsi, à l'instar de nombreux autres pays européens, la constitution de la RFA prévoit un véritable statut des cultes incluant une protection de la liberté d'organisation interne: «Chaque Église ou société religieuse règle et administre ses affaires de façon autonome dans les limites de la législation valable pour tous. Elles confèrent leurs charges sans intervention de l'État» (Art. 140 GG/Art. 137 Abs 3 WRV). En revanche, la constitution française du 4 octobre 1958 limite ses garanties aux libertés individuelle et collective de religion dans le cadre du principe de neutralité et de non-confessionnalité de l'État (laïcité) ainsi que de la liberté d'opinion. Les cultes s'organisent conformément à la loi de Germinal an X (droit local alsacien-mosellan) et à la loi du 9 décembre 1905 (droit général). Aucun de ces deux systèmes ne prévoit une protection explicite de la liberté institutionnelle des Églises.

La libre organisation interne des cultes peut toutefois être considérée comme un principe général du droit français défini par la jurisprudence administrative à l'occasion des conflits faisant suite à la loi de séparation de 1905. En droit local alsacien-mosellan elle est encore limitée par toute une série de textes qui institutionnalisent une immixtion de l'État dans la quasi-totalité des affaires relevant des collectivités religieuses (fixation des circonscriptions religieuses, nomination des ministres du culte). Notons que dans ce dernier cas l'intervention de la puissance publique, due à l'obsolescence des textes plus qu'à une volonté de l'État, a un caractère purement formel.

De plus le système français est caractérisé par la «spécialisation cultuelle» en matière religieuse. L'autocompréhension des Églises et religions est limitée par la législation étatique aux seules activités dites cultuelles au sens large du terme (exercice du culte, transmission de la foi, formation et entretien des ministres du culte, etc.). Les activités socio-caritatives et éducatives, qui ne sont pas des activités propres de l'Église relèvent du droit commun. Lorsqu'elles sont en lien avec des Églises et religions, les institutions ou associations gestionnaires de ces activités sont considérées comme étant des entreprises de tendance, dont les employés sont soumis au principe de loyauté.

Différente est la situation allemande où la Cour constitutionnelle fédérale reconnaît aux Églises le droit de déterminer le type d'activité relevant de leur mission. Il s'agit le plus souvent d'activités socio-caritatives, hospitalières et éducatives. Les Églises développent, par ailleurs, leurs propres normes, sous le contrôle du juge; dans le cadre du droit étatique du travail en fixant les devoirs de leurs employés. Les Églises et religions en RFA ne sont pas uniquement des entreprises de tendance. Elles font l'objet d'une qualification spécifique, celle de communauté de service dont les employés sont associés à la mission spirituelle de l'employeur.

2. La représentativité des religions

La religion n'a qu'une place minorée au sein des institutions en France. En effet, les religions organisées ne sont pas investies de la même représentativité que les autres groupes intermédiaires et cela malgré toute la discussion autour de la représentativité du culte musulman. Il conviendrait dans ce cas plutôt de parler d'organisation centralisée du culte musulman ou de représentativité d'un culte par rapport à l'État plutôt que de sa représentativité dans l'État. Il en va différemment de la RFA où les grandes Églises et religions occupent une place particulière dans la sphère publique.

Leur rôle social est reconnu par plusieurs constitutions d'États fédérés. Le système de coopération est formalisé par l'utilisation quasi-systématique du droit conventionnel pour régler les relations entre les États fédérés et les religions. Enfin l'action publique (*Öffentlichkeitsauftrag*) des grandes Églises est consacrée par les textes. Elles agissent ostensiblement et peuvent interpeller la société civile et le pouvoir politique.

Cette reconnaissance de la place publique des religions a des conséquences institutionnelles. Ainsi ce sont les autorités religieuses qui nomment à la demande de l'administration les membres représentant les Églises dans les divers comités consultatifs. En France, c'est le pouvoir politique qui choisit un ecclésiastique considéré comme étant représentatif de sa collectivité sans demander un avis formel aux chefs de la religion concernée (comité national d'éthique, mission du dialogue en Nouvelle Calédonie, Conseil national du SIDA).

Toutefois, même en France la puissance publique reconnaît sans le dire la contribution des grandes Églises et religions à l'intérêt général. A l'instar des groupes intermédiaires reconnus d'utilité publique, les Églises et religions (associations cultuelles et diocésaines) peuvent se constituer en associations ayant la grande capacité et bénéficier des mêmes exonérations fiscales. Mais contrairement à l'Italie et à la RFA, les Églises n'ont pas un statut d'autonomie. La «coopération» entre les deux institutions ne s'opère donc pas au même niveau.

3. Les modes de production du droit

La prise ou non en compte de la liberté d'organisation des Églises et de leur auto-compréhension ainsi que leur place dans la société et l'État n'est pas sans lien avec les modes de production du droit appliqué aux cultes. La France (droit général et droits locaux) est un pays de droit unilatéral. Les textes s'appliquant aux institutions cultuelles et au clergé sont certes négociés informellement mais souvent avec les représentants de la seule Église catholique en l'absence de référence à des principes généraux clairement définis. La France contemporaine n'est pas en matière religieuse un pays de droit conventionnel. Les exceptions du Concordat du 15 juillet 1801 et des conventions du 5 décembre 1902 et du 25 mai 1974 fixant le statut de la faculté de théologie catholique de Strasbourg et du centre autonome de pédagogie religieuse de Metz ne font que confirmer cette règle. Le concordat de 1801 précisant notamment la procédure de nomination des évêques par le chef de l'État n'a jamais été retouché et les conventions de 1902 et de 1974 n'ont pas été publiées. Elles ne sont donc pas opposables à un tiers en cas de recours devant une juridiction administrative.

Inversement, en RFA, mais également dans d'autres pays comme l'Italie et l'Espagne, toutes les matières dites mixtes font l'objet de négociations et aboutissent à la signature de conventions relevant du droit international pour l'Église catholique ou de conventions de droit public interne pour les autres grandes Églises et religions.

4. Enseignement religieux et transmission de la culture religieuse

Une autre illustration de la fonction diversifiée de la religion institutionnalisée dans les sociétés française et allemande est celle de l'enseignement religieux et plus largement de la transmission de la culture religieuse à l'école.

La question du déficit en matière de culture religieuse des élèves du primaire et du secondaire s'est en France transformée en débat national. En Vieille-France (droit général), le droit à l'enseignement religieux a toujours été pensé en termes de liberté de culte et de conscience qui sont des droits individuels.

Pour les réaliser, les parents disposent d'une journée libre par semaine dans les établissements primaires, qui sont par ailleurs interdits d'accès à tout personnel ayant un caractère religieux. Par ailleurs, les parents et eux seuls peuvent demander la création d'une «aumônerie» mais non pas d'un cours d'enseignement religieux au sein des établissements secondaires. Les Églises ne prennent aucune initiative et se contentent de nommer l'aumônier laïc ou clerc.

En droit local alsacien-mosellan, le cadre juridique est certes différent et les cours de religion sont organisés au sein des établissements primaires et secondaires de concert avec les quatre cultes reconnus. Mais ces cours sont considérés avant tout comme une activité de type pastoral sans véritable articulation avec les autres matières fixées par les programmes scolaires. Ce caractère marginal est actuellement remis en question. Les divers acteurs sociaux réfléchissent à la création d'un CAPES de religion (concours national prévu pour le recrutement de tous les enseignants dans le cadre du statut général de la fonction publique) et à la mise en place de modules intégrant la culture ou la connaissance religieuse.

En RFA l'enseignement religieux est garanti par l'article 7 de la loi fondamentale. Dispensé sous le contrôle des Églises, il comprend un volet culturel ou d'histoire et de connaissance des religions. Les enseignants de religion ont le même statut que les autres enseignants et leur enseignement est noté. Il peut être choisi comme une des matières du diplôme de fin d'études/*Abitur*.

Conclusion

Les relations entre les États et les religions en Europe sont régies par des systèmes sociaux et politiques très fortement marqués par l'histoire. Il serait donc vain actuellement de chercher un lien quelconque entre l'expression des sentiments religieux collectifs et la particularité d'un régime des cultes. L'intensité de la religiosité[1] ou inversement sa faiblesse ou son absence n'a que peu d'influence sur le statut des cultes et le droit des religions en général.

Ce constat ne manque pas d'interroger sur de probables évolutions futures des relations entre État et religions. L'Europe est dans sa grande majorité confrontée à des situations nouvelles: sécularisation de la société, individualisation des convictions religieuses, émergence et affirmation d'autres religions que celles implantées historiquement, alors que les structures actuelles des statuts cultuels ont vu le jour dans un contexte d'homogénéité sociale et confessionnelle. Partant de cette problématique commune, une réflexion universitaire sur la place des Églises et religions dans le cadre de l'Union européenne devrait à mon sens être tout particulièrement attentive:

1. A la prise en compte des différents régimes des cultes existant en Europe, y compris ceux peu connus ou considérés comme marginaux.

2. Aux besoins spécifiques de l'Islam, des religions orientales et des minorités religieuses en général. L'hypothèse d'un renforcement de la coopération des grandes religions historiques avec les institutions de l'Union européenne ne devrait pas occulter la démarche dite des droits fondamentaux. La liberté de religion, incluant la libre organisation interne, doit être accessible à tous les groupements respectant l'ordre public.

3. A la demande sociale en la matière. Si les rapports entre les religions et l'Union européenne ne peuvent certes pas se régler par référendum, il reste qu'un minimum d'attention à la sensibilité des populations en ce domaine paraît nécessaire.

---

[1] Voir à ce sujet Y. LAMBERT, «Les régimes confessionnels et l'état du sentiment religieux», in *Religions et laïcité dans l'Europe des douze,* dir. J. BAUBÉROT, Paris, Syros, 1994, p. 241-272.

EUROPEAN COMMUNITY LAW AND CHURCHES

Gerhard ROBBERS

I

European law knows but feeble hints to the position of churches and religious communities. Established on primarily economic and general political aspects, churches did from the very beginning not come into the horizon of European legal thinking. Churches may, as part of activities within society, be regarded by European law as existing - special recognition of their relevance, acknowledgement of their special needs is off the mainstream of European law.

Nevertheless, there are some hints within this legal system, on which churches can rely - thin enough, not firm ground to exist on.

II

In primarily law, art. F. section 2 makes the fundamental rights as guaranteed by the European convention on fundamental rights a part of community law. Among these fundamental rights we find religious freedom guaranteed in art. 9 of the convention. Certainly, religious freedom is one of the foremost rights guaranteeing the existence and the free development of religious communities within society. On the other hand, the guarantee of fundamental rights as stated in art. F section 2 TUV remains somewhat indirect, not completely integrated within the context of European law.

Furthermore, this guarantee starts from the individual performance of religious needs. It is a right of the individual, only in the second place a right of the institution as far as legal development has come up until today. Though we witness a process within the jurisdiction of the European Court of Human Rights in Strasbourg to the acknowledgement of institutional rights within the idea of religious freedom, we cannot be sure that this structure will be accepted in the long run as integral part of the guarantee of art. 9 of the convention. Hopefully enough, since institutional rights of the churches are part of many a European constitution, not the least also part of the traditional development of religious existence in Europe, we can expect that this juridiction of the European

Court of Human Rights will go on finding its path to one of the roots of
the fundamental human rights within European history.

It is but an almost logical consequence, that also European institutions, especially the European Court of Justice of Luxembourg, will join
in this development and accept art. 9 of the European Convention of
Fundamental Rights as being a source of institutional rights of religious
communities within European law. As such, it would be one of the most
important legal provisions to guarantee the autonomy of the churches.
To what extent and with what meaning this autonomy would be
accepted will, though, still have to be argued.

The idea of the legal tradition within Europe gives rise to a second link
in European law to the standing of religious institutions. The European
Court of Justice in Luxembourg as well as the treaty on European Union
itself have developed the legal principle of "the common constitutional
traditions of the member states". Most certainly, those common constitutional traditions of the member states do include religious freedom on the
one hand side as an individual right, as well as institutional structures on
the other hand side. Quite certainly, the autonomy of the churches, their
right to decide freely on the contents of their beliefs and also on the fields
of religious actions is maintained within these common constitutional traditions. Notwithstanding the fact, that each one of the member states of
the European Union does have its own, often in itself divers, system of
state church relationships. Freedom of religion and church autonomy is
known to all these systems. This holds true even for those states who do
know a state church. Also within these systems, churches who do not
want to follow the path of a state church, would be free to do so.

We do have to see, however, that this notion of common constitutional traditions is but a rather general idea yet to be brought down to
earth and to concrete meaning by future jurisdiction and legal thinking.
We cannot be sure today, that well accepted and reasonable structures
within the member states of the European Union will find their way into
the European legal system as such. What has been fought for and gained
within member states legal systems, will have to be fought for and
gained in the future still within European law.

III

Further acknowledgements of religious needs can be found in secondary community law. The television directive holds, that commercials
within TV-programmes may not impede religious feelings. Religious

programmes like the broadcasting of services may not be interrupted by advertisements. Though this may seem to be a question somewhat off the core of church interests, we should not underestimate its relevance. Secondary community law has in this case openly and expressly accepted religious need to be respected. It can be taken as an example to be followed within future legal reasoning on this level.

A further step is being undertaken in the draft directive on personal data protection. Here, special need of religious communities to collect and process personal data not only of their members have been accepted as forming part of public interests within the member states.

Finally, not least, the European Court of Justice has in its jurisdiction accepted religious interests as forming relevant guidelines to actions of European institutions. Within the famous case Praise v. Council the plaintiff objected to having been obliged to sit a test on a day forming a religious holiday for him. The European Court of Justice held, that religious needs have to be taken into account by European institutions, and that they have to organise as far as possible their activities in order to impede with this needs.

We have to note, though, that the European Court of Justice speaks of religious interests only. It does not, as yet, speak of religious freedom or of the fundamental right to religious activities. In the terms of legal history, this must be regarded with some suspicion. It does not live up to the importance and predominant role of religious freedom within the development of the European and Anglo-American idea of fundamental rights.

IV

It does seem, that although we do find certain hints on religious needs within community law which can and must be further developed, this development should be based on an expressed acknowledgement of these interests. Religious interests must be given a solid legal basis within the instruments of the European Union. Not only as a matter of individual rights, but also as a matter of institutional existence of these needs. Religion, historically as well as in the consequence of its very social structures from today, must be regarded as a matter of institutions.

Thus, there is an obvious need to place a provision within the instruments on the European Union which guarantees the existence, the role and the rights of religious institutions. This should not be done by developing a new, European wide system of state-church relationships.

Accepting that state-church relationships form a very intens part of national and regional identities, of history and culture of member states, the existing systems of state church relationships within the member states should be guaranteed by European law. Thus, the community should respect the constitutional position of the religious communities within the member states as an expression of the national identity of the member states and their cultures. Certainly, religious communities should form part of European integration in the sense of helping to develop and to keep up a European identity, to guard the process of European politics. This has been the role of religious communities since long; the common cultural heritage can not be understood without the contribution of the religious communities. From this point of view, the most different systems of state church relationships within the member states of the European Union do form part of the European common cultural heritage to be developed and safeguarded as a treasure for the further development of European society. All this together must form part of European law itself. It is not to outcast a certain field of law from the development of the European Union. It is to maintain accepted and lively areas of social life as an integral part of European legal development. It is also not to petrify existing legal structures within the member states. They can experience their own lively future structuring. As part of European law this respect of constitutional features within the member states will find a guideline within religious freedom as guaranteed by art. 9 of the European Convention on Human Rights and art. F section 2 TUV.

LE CADRE SOCIAL.

LES EGLISES ET L'ETAT DANS LEURS RAPPORTS VIS-À-VIS DES PROBLÈMES SOCIAUX ACTUELS

Theodor Strohm / Britta von Schubert

Thèse d'introduction sur la question du droit européen Eglises-Etat :

Toute réflexion au sujet d'une détermination législative des relations entre l'Union Européenne et les Eglises en Europe doit être accompagnée d'une réflexion au sujet de la mission et de la responsabilité de l'Eglise.

La diversité des systèmes du droit Eglises-Etat dans les Etats membres pourrait séduire les partenaires de tout simplement essayer de fixer le statu quo du système national en question. Le développement actuel aussi bien que le chemin à faire dans l'avenir pour arriver à l'unification européenne posent la question de savoir quels pas les Eglises vont faire sur ce chemin.

De même faut-il éviter le danger de minimaliser la contribution des Eglises européennes à un développement profitable pour tous par le fait que l'on cherche le plus petit dénominateur commun dans les différents systèmes Eglises-Etat.

Comme point de départ d'une fixation du droit Eglises-Etat dans l'avenir il faut accorder priorité à la question de savoir comment trouver un chemin commun et une responsabilité commune des Eglises en Europe. En rapport avec ceci il faut se rappeler que l'idée fondamentale du principe de subsidiarité, ancré dans le traité de Maastricht, ne consiste pas à fixer des délimitations et des compétences, mais à inviter les partenaires à coopérer pour arriver à une coopération qui soit secourable et qui résoud les problèmes. Il est de la mission des Eglises de lier le service du prochain au service de la communauté et du bien public. Ceci ne se réduit plus aujourd'hui au cadre national, mais doit être compris dans le cadre européen et mondial.

D'autre part le fait n'est pas contesté que l'Europe moderne n'est pas seulement caractérisée par la pluralité de ses nations, mais aussi par ses scissions confessionnelles, par la pluralité des Eglises et des

confessions. Avec l'intention d'une opposition délibérée et voulue
contre les scissions confessionnelles — effectuées par la Réformation —
une Europe nouvelle s'est formée, résultat d'un processus d'émancipa-
tion et de sécularisation. Sous sa forme de rationalité spécifique et des
sciences, de sa technologie et de son économie, cette Europe s'est trans-
férée dans le monde entier et elle est omniprésente dans la réalité du
monde actuel. Il n'est donc pas surprenant que l'Union Européenne soit
en premier lieu une communauté économique, technologique, monétaire,
une communauté d'armement et de défense, et que, en deuxième et
troisième lieu seulement, elle puisse être appelée une communauté cul-
turelle, politique et sociale. Jusqu'à présent les Eglises n'ont pas été les
forces d'impulsion les plus importantes. Si l'ordre européen ne doit pas
se raidir dans un système de structures macro-économiques guidé d'une
manière technocrate et burocratique, alors il faut y ajouter les traditions
culturelles et religieuses de l'histoire. Le Cardinal Joseph Ratzinger a
expliqué dans sa conférence lors du symposion «Eglise et Economie» à
Rome en 1986:

> «Il devient de plus en plus clair historiquement que la formation des
> systèmes économiques et leur fondement dans le bien public dépendent
> d'une discipline éthique précise qui, de sa part, ne peut être formulée
> que par des puissances religieuses. Il devient également apparent
> qu'inversement le déclin d'une telle discipline fait effondrer les lois du
> marché. Une politique économique qui ne correspond pas seulement
> au bien d'un groupe, pas seulement au bien public d'un seul Etat,
> mais aussi au bien public de toute la famille humaine, cela exige une
> éthique extrêmement disciplinée et une puissance religieuse extraor-
> dinaire. La formation d'une volonté politique qui se sert des lois éco-
> nomiques en vue de ce but, paraît aujourd'hui presqu'impossible;
> elle ne peut être réalisée que si de nouvelles puissances éthiques appa-
> raissent.»

Dans la suite il va être nécessaire de mettre l'accent sur quelques
problèmes qui se trouvent à l'ordre du jour en vue d'une meilleure
coopération et d'un meilleur accord entre les Eglises en Europe. En
outre, quelques terrains seront mentionnés sur lesquels une coopération
a été commencée, et quelques perspectives en vue d'un service plus
étendu seront soulignées.

1. Quelques remarques à propos des approches confessionnelle et juridique des questions posées

1.1. Les empreintes confessionnelles qu'on trouve dans les systèmes sociaux

Dans le passé, les confessions avaient une fonction qui a laissé des empreintes sur la formation du système social en question. C'est l'historien Gerhard Uhlhorn qui, en 1894, a pu distinguer trois approches différentes pour régler les relations entre les oeuvres diaconales des Eglises et l'ordre de l'Etat.

> «C'est catholique de réclamer le soin des pauvres pour l'Eglise et de déléguer à l'Etat seulement la tâche de soutenir l'Eglise là, où ses activités ne sont pas suffisantes.
>
> C'est réformé de séparer l'Eglise et l'Etat de sorte que leurs soins pour les pauvres sont portés d'un esprit différent.
>
> C'est luthérien de laisser à l'Etat le soin pour les pauvres, mais de pénétrer ce soin ainsi que l'Etat en entier d'un esprit chrétien et de le soutenir par une charité libre pour qu'il puisse accomplir ses tâches.»

Dans ce contexte relativement restreint il n'a pas encore été question des Eglises orthodoxes. Il correspond aux traditions orthodoxes de transférer les tâches micro-diaconiques — conséquence immédiate de la liturgie — dans les structures d'une vie commune entre voisins, entre frères et soeurs, tandis que les tâches macro-diaconiques, ainsi que par exemple les systèmes modernes de sécurité, ont été déléguées à l'Etat. Dans le mouvement européen du réveil du 19ème et du 20ème siècle de nouvelles formes d'aide sociale se sont développées ainsi que dans le méthodisme anglo-saxon, dans le mouvement des quakers ou dans «l'armée du salut», tous des mouvements d'une foi chrétienne de l'action et des droits fondamentaux humains qui avaient déployé leurs activités dans les centres de détresse sociale. Ils ont ajouté beaucoup au renouvellement de la responsabilité des Eglises en Europe.

1.2. De différentes approches vues du droit des Eglises

Les Eglises d'Europe se trouvent dans de différents systèmes de droit Etat-Eglise. En France l'Eglise catholique aussi bien que l'Eglise protestante sont séparées de l'Etat et les Eglises sont responsables de la situation financière de leur travail et de leurs collaborateurs (sauf en Alsace-Lorraine où on trouve une plus grande proximité Etat-Eglise). Les Eglises scandinaves sont jusqu'à présent des Eglises d'Etat. En

Allemagne les deux Eglises sont des sociétés (des collectivités) de droit
public, munies de nombreux privilèges (impôt ecclésiastique, dotations
de l'Etat etc.) et, comme représentants des questions sociales, elles sont
responsables de l'organisation de l'aménagement social avec priorité et
d'après les principes de parité confessionnelle. Dans les systèmes des
Eglises d'Etat de la Scandinavie les Eglises surtout luthériennes ont remis
aux responsables de l'Etat les compétences pour l'aménagement social.
En même temps elles se sont concentrées sur la diaconie à l'intérieur des
paroisses et sur la libre coopération avec l'Etat social. La France comme
Etat laïque connaît de nombreuses associations d'aide sociale (environ
90 000 associations privées, parmi lesquelles 1000 vraiment grandes),
mais l'Etat n'a pas de liaison étroite avec les prestataires ecclésiastiques
et religieux comme en Allemagne. Même en Italie et en Espagne le travail social libre est indépendant de l'Etat et il est toujours exécuté par des
«volontari», des collaborateurs volontaires locaux. Les conséquences de
cette diversité dans les systèmes Etat-Eglises en vue de l'organisation du
système social en question sont évidentes. En vue des Eglises en Allemagne on a fixé avant Maastricht des principes qui, en partie, sont entrés
dans le traité de Maastricht. De la part des Eglises on a précisé:

> «Les objectifs d'une politique allemande en vue de l'Union Européenne
> devraient être:
>
> — une garantie aussi étendue que possible d'une coopération de tous les
>   groupes de la société et surtout des Eglises à toutes les affaires
>   publiques dans la Communauté, sur tous les niveaux de décisions à
>   prendre et de leur préparation,
>
> — l'introduction et la garantie juridique du principe de subsidiarité dans
>   la Communauté quand il s'agit de l'expédition des affaires courantes,
>   non seulement sur le plan de la Communauté et des Etats membres,
>   mais aussi pour les pays et les régions aussi bien que pour les organi-
>   sations et les institutions de la société et des Eglises,
>
> — l'adoption du principe fédéral dans la communauté; ici joint le res-
>   pect des compétences données aux pays membres pour régler leurs
>   relations avec les Eglises.»

1.3. *Les systèmes existants de la sécurité sociale et les Eglises en Europe.*

Dans les pays de l'Union Européenne il y a au moins quatre systèmes
de sécurité sociale tout à fait différents. Aujourd'hui tous les systèmes
touchent à leurs bornes qui peuvent être surmontées par l'invention de
structures innovatrices et transnationales.

Le modèle d'assurance sociale tel qu'il existe en Allemagne et en Europe continentale: systèmes d'assurance généraux obligatoires pour certaines catégories professionnelles et garantissant le statut social sur la base de cotisations et de subventions publiques (modèle dit de Bismarck).

Le modèle anglais (dénommé d'après Lord Beveridge, 1942): sécurité générale uniforme par des prestations publiques venant des recettes fiscales; le niveau de prestation est calculé au plus juste et vise à parer aux situations de détresse par l'application des deux principes de l'assurance sociale d'une part et de l'aide sociale d'autre part.

Le modèle scandinave: institutions de sécurité générales et uniformes avec un niveau de prestation substantiel et des services sociaux aménagés; couverture sociale maximale par «l'état providence» grâce aux moyens fiscaux.

Le modèle des Etats d'Europe méridionale y compris la Grèce: système rudimentaire d'«assistance publique», partiellement sans droit reconnu à l'aide sociale. En substitution aux prestations et aux institutions sociales des organismes privés et publics, c'est bien souvent encore la famille, le «clan», ainsi que l'Eglise catholique et ses prestations sociales variées dans les pays latins qui jouent le rôle important de réseau social. Toutefois, on observe actuellement une forte mutation.

2. Les églises en Europe devant de nouveaux défis et devant la tâche d'une coopération croissante.

2.1. *Surmonter lentement la position défensive vis-à-vis des changements rapides dans le domaine social et vis-à-vis de la sécularisation croissante.*

Pendant les dernières dizaines d'années les Eglises européennes ont contribué en grande mesure à critiquer les systèmes sociaux dans les pays membres et à coopérer pour surmonter les insuffisances dans leurs structures. Il faut penser par exemple au large processus d'études «Faith in the city» de la Church of England; aux «Denkschriften» de l'Eglise Protestante en Allemagne au sujet de «l'organisation nouvelle de la sécurité sociale des personnes âgées», et aussi au sujet de «la solidarité entre ceux qui ont et ceux qui n'ont pas d'emploi» et au sujet d'une réorganisation du système de la santé. L'Eglise catholique a mené un large processus de réflexions au sujet d'une «Nouvelle Evangélisation de l'Europe». Un extrait du discours du Pape Jean-Paul II lors du symposium de 1982 en est caractéristique.

Il y dit son avis sur la question de savoir quelle contribution les églises doivent apporter en Europe. A son avis, nous devons comprendre les défis actuels en même temps que nous annonçons l'Evangile, «... la famille, la jeunesse, les zones de pauvreté et les pauvres en Europe, les minorités ethniques et religieuses, les relations entre l'Europe et le Tiers Monde. Si nous parlons de la Foi et de la Sainteté de l'Eglise pour répondre à ces problèmes et à ces défis, ce n'est pas parce que nous voulons avoir ou regagner le pouvoir, mais nous nous croyons obligés de connaitre les causes des défis et des problèmes.»

On ne peut pas douter connaître du sérieux de ces phrases. L'Eglise Protestante en Allemagne (EKD) a publié un texte d'experts (Denkschrift) sous le titre «Responsables d'une Europe sociale» (Gütersloh 1991). Ce texte présente les dimensions d'une responsabilité future des Eglises pour l'aménagement social en Europe.

2.2. L'effort que font les Eglises afin de répondre aux défis sociaux actuels

Un évènement important a été les assemblées oecuméniques à Bâle et à Seoul, que toutes les Eglises européennes s'étaient proposées de réaliser. Le but en avait été de formuler des déclarations unanimes au sujet de la justice, de la paix et de la protection de la création et de trouver un accord sur les principes suivants:

«S'engager en faveur de la vie: Dieu préserve et aime toute l'humanité et appelle ses créatures à être les intendants de ce monde dont il est le seul propriétaire. Cela donne à toute l'humanité, y compris aux réfugiés et aux demandeurs d'asile, un espoir immense concernant la défense et la protection du droit fondamental à la vie. S'engager en faveur de la vie, c'est aussi travailler à l'avènement d'une société où tous ont les mêmes droits et vivent ensemble.

Travailler pour la justice et la paix: lorsqu'on fait partie des enfants de Dieu le Créateur, le Libérateur, du Dieu de justice (Mt 5; 6,10; Luc 4,18 et 19) on ne peut que plaider vigoureusement la cause des marginalisés, dont font partie les réfugiés et les demandeurs d'asile, et défendre leur dignité. La protection et la défense de la dignité humaine font partie du témoignage de l'Eglise.

Etre porteurs du message d'unité et de solidarité: de même que Jésus a proclamé et manifesté l'unité et la solidarité au monde des humains, de même les chrétiens sont appelés à porter à leur tour le même message à l'humanité dont font partie les réfugiés et les demandeurs d'asile, souvent dans la détresse. C'est pourquoi celui ou celle qui porte le message de l'unité et de la solidarité du Christ ne peut que s'engager activement, par une action cohérente et coordonnée, sur le terrain de l'asile et de la défense des réfugiés (Rm 5,1-3).

On ne peut le faire qu'en respectant et en réalisant intégralement les droits fondamentaux de l'homme. Pour porter le message d'unité et de solidarité du Christ, les chrétiens doivent assumer pleinement leurs responsabilités séculières, légales et religieuses et ce, même lorsqu'ils s'occupent directement des réfugiés et des demandeurs d'asile.»

2.3. Exemple I: les problèmes des réfugiés et de l'asile

Un premier exemple d'une responsabilité ecclésiastique en Europe est donné par le problème des réfugiés et par la question de l'asile. Les Eglises en Europe ont commencé à s'occuper de ces problèmes de deux façons différentes: elles redécouvrent la tradition du ainsi-dit «asile d'église» et offrent par là une protection contre l'expulsion non-justifiée. Elles font l'effort d'arriver à une volonté commune à propos de cette «question des étrangers et des réfugiés». Exemple: «Déclaration commune de la conférence Justitia et Pax et du comité des Eglises pour les questions des étrangers en Europe», du 27 juin 1991. Des réglementations obligatoires pour l'intégration des immigrés dans les pays de l'Europe y sont exigées. Au mois de mars 1988 «le groupe de travail des Eglises européennes pour l'asile et les réfugiés» (ECWGAR) a été constitué, action commune de la Conférence des Eglises Européennes (CEE) et de la «Commission du Conseil Oecuménique des Eglises d'entraide ecclésiastique, de réfugiés et de service d'asile» (CICARWS). Sa mission consiste à poursuivre, à rendre public et à réviser les activités des groupes TREVI et Schengen en ce qui concerne les droits fondamentaux humains. Ni le Haut-Commissaire de l'ONU pour les réfugiés ni aucune autre organisation non-gouvernementale n'avait eu la permission ni d'observer ces discussions des gouvernements ni d'y prendre part. Cela veut dire que les Eglises en Europe commencent à avoir une «fonction de garde prophétique» jusqu'à la limite d'une «résistance civile» exigée, et cela peut avoir des conséquences de grande portée.

2.4. Exemple II: le racisme

En Allemagne, le thème du racisme était devenu d'une actualité imminente à l'époque du nazisme. La politique raciste avait fait souffrir incroyablement des peuples entiers. Les Eglises en Allemagne se sont gravement rendues coupables par leur manque d'attitude résolue, leur réserve vis-à-vis de la politique de l'holocauste. Il faut remarquer qu'en 1872 déjà l'Eglise orthodoxe par ses représentants officiels (Synode du

Patriarche) avait adopté une résolution claire contre le racisme et le nationalisme. Avec des déclarations nombreuses les Eglises chrétiennes se sont engagées à s'opposer avec vigueur à toute sorte de racisme. Ainsi par exemple dans l'engagement de Lausanne du mouvement mondial d'évangélisation en 1980 (engagement V). En outre la conférence mondiale oecuménique à Uppsala en 1968 a constaté:

> «L'homme a été renouvelé en Christ. C'est au nom de cette vérité que nous devons juger et répudier les déformations tragiques de l'humanité dans l'existence des hommes, et dont certaines se manifestent même dans la communauté chrétienne. Malgré tous leurs sermons contre le racisme, on trouve encore dans des Eglises des pratiques de ségrégation raciale, à tel point que certains se voient refoulés à cause de la couleur de leur peau, alors même que ces Eglises se réunissent au nom du Christ. Un tel déni de la catholicité doit être condamné sans délai et avec la plus grande énergie. «Jusqu'à quand, Seigneur, jusqu'à quand?» Le renouveau doit apparaître d'abord dans la communauté locale: il faut y repérer et en extirper tout exclusivisme racial ou social, y lutter contre toute dégradation et toute exploitation économique, politique et sociale de l'homme.»

2.5. Exemple III: la pauvreté et la marginalisation

Ce n'est pas par hasard que, dans leurs programmes d'action pour l'intégration des handicapés HELIOS I, II et pour la lutte contre la pauvreté et la marginalisation (Poverty I-III), la Communauté Européenne soit partie, ici et là, de quelques initiatives de groupes chrétiens. Surtout les trois programmes concernant la pauvreté se sont référés à des expériences qu'avaient faites des initiatives extraordinaires de groupes chrétiens. En premier lieu il faut penser aux activités de l'abbé Pierre, père des pauvres et des sans-abris en France. Mais il faut souligner aussi l'engagement du père Joseph Wresinski qui a donné vie au «mouvement du quart monde» et qui, en 1987, a présenté un rapport de pauvreté au nom du conseil économique et social français. Actuellement les rapports de pauvreté et les programmes de pauvreté font chemin en Europe main dans la main. Le troisième «programme d'action de la Communauté pour l'intégration des groupes les plus désavantagés» s'attribue de montrer comment on peut trouver, sur le plan régional, national et européen, des chemins nouveaux pour lutter contre la pauvreté. Il faut constater que c'est l'Allemagne qui, malheureusement, s'est engagée à ne plus poursuivre ce programme et qui l'a arrêté. Les trois programmes d'action pour l'intégration des handicapés suivent le même chemin. Leur but consiste à trouver les conditions et les perspectives d'intégration par l'échange intensif d'idées innovatrices dans des réseaux européens. Tous les projets sont financés d'une façon commune (de 50 à 75 % par la Commission). Les projets sont en partie réalisés par «les oeuvres de bienfaisance qui ont déjà trouvé leur place dans le système social (ATC, Caritas etc.)». Les Eglises pourraient y découvrir des possibilités d'une coopération et d'un dialogue au-delà des frontières pour trouver la meilleure réalisation de leurs buts sociaux.

Dans ce contexte la tâche qui se pose tout aussi bien aux Etats qu'aux Eglises dans l'Union Européenne est évidente. Elle consiste à développer des initiatives communes pour vaincre le problème mondial de la pauvreté. Il ne s'agit pas seulement de développer des modèles de travail communs et intégrés, mais aussi de faire «des efforts pour créer un modèle des rapports entre pays développés et pays en développement en vue d'un ordre économique plus juste et mieux équilibré dans le monde» (Art. 1 Lomé IV).

3. Possibilités d'élaborer de nouvelles formes institutionnelles d'une coopération des Eglises en vue de la formation d'un nouvel aménagement social en Europe.

3.1. Exemples d'une participation de l'Eglise (et de sa diaconie/caritas) aux institutions de la Communauté Européenne.

Les grandes Eglises chrétiennes ont établi une multitude de représentations politico-sociales à Bruxelles et à Strasbourg. A côté des représentations officielles des Eglises — catholique, protestante et orthodoxe — il y a surtout six bureaux importants qu'on devrait nommer:

— Comité des Eglises auprès des Migrants en Europe (CEME)
— European Ecumenical Organization for Development (EECOD)
— European Ecumenical Commission for Church and Society (EECCS)
— Federazione Organismi Christiani di Servizio Volontario (FOCSIV)
— Vertretung der Bundesarbeitsgemeinschaft der Freien Wohlfahrtspflege e.V.
— Réseau Sud-Nord Cultures et Développement
— Commission des Episcopats de la Communauté Européenne (COMECE)

Leurs intentions consistent à mettre en valeur auprès des organes de la Commission ce qui leur semble important. Le regroupement fédéral allemand de la libre bienfaisance a insisté sur sa participation à droits égaux au «comité économique et social de la Commission» et elle l'a réalisée.

3.2. *Trouver des perspectives communes dans l'Etat et dans l'Eglise en vue d'une Europe sociale!*

Les tendances existantes permettent de distinguer des perspectives à long terme. Elles peuvent être considérées comme des conditions nécessaires pour créer une Union Européenne sociale et homogène. Ce qui existe déjà dans ce domaine doit être poussé en avant. L'harmonisation graduelle des différents systèmes du droit du travail ainsi que des systèmes de la sécurité sociale sont des pas sur ce chemin. L'Europe en tant qu'état social sera fondé sur les principes du droit social et du droit du travail dans le cadre de l'économie du marché social et sur la coopération des syndicats et des associations économiques, des partenaires sociaux, des représentants des assurances sociales et de ses organes, des pays fédéraux, des communes, des représentants libres, des Eglises et du grand nombre de citoyens travaillant à titre professionnel ou bénévole. Ainsi l'Etat social contribuerait graduellement à l'établissement de conditions de vie homogènes dans l'Europe unie. Ce but peut être atteint grâce à une *coopération* subsidiaire des pouvoirs, non par une *délimitation* subsidiaire.

Les Eglises devraient être les moteurs d'une intégration européenne dans laquelle les meilleures traditions culturelles et ethico-sociales des différents pays et des différentes confessions entrent dans un échange productif et contribuent à la formation d'une volonté politique. Ce développement se caractérise par un esprit d'ouverture à l'intérieur et à l'extérieur. Il faut absolument s'opposer à toute fermeture de l'Union Européenne.

Il est du devoir des Eglises de rappeler au gouvernement le but éthique de la politique et de faire cela dans un esprit de solidarité critique et constructive, en coopération avec les institutions de l'Etat social qui seraient de plus en plus démocratiquement légitimées. Cela veut dire qu'elles s'engagent à offrir, à garantir et à développer, d'une façon dynamique, des possibilités de vivre pour leurs habitants. La constitution de l'Union Européenne doit s'orienter vers un Etat social qui aide les pauvres, qui organise la participation aux biens économiques d'après les principes de la justice, tout ceci pour garantir une vie dans la dignité humaine à chaque personne. Afin de réaliser ce but, la patience doit aller de pair avec une disposition à la communication et à la coopération.

3.3. *Développer en commun des stratégies et des modèles d'action!*

Dans ces perspectives pour l'avenir, six points sont à signaler.

3.3.1. Jusqu'à l'an 2000 les rapports oecuméniques devraient être élargis pour arriver à des formes de coopération dans tous les domaines concernant les droits fondamentaux de l'homme et leur violation, la garantie de la dignité humaine et la réalisation de la justice sociale. Lors de la conférence des Eglises européennes (CEE) «Vers une vision de la diaconie en Europe» (Bratislava, octobre 1994) cinq tâches ont été nommées:

> «La diaconie, aspect essentiel du christianisme,
>
> — est au service des hommes et des femmes dans leur vie quotidienne, lorsqu'ils sont confrontés, par exemple, à la maladie, la faim, la vieillesse, le deuil, leur apportant l'aide matérielle et spirituelle nécessaire;
>
> — est la liturgie après la liturgie, c'est-à-dire le prolongement du culte et de l'adoration dans la vie courante, engageant l'ensemble du peuple de Dieu;
>
> — contribue activement et dans un esprit créateur à l'édification de la communauté humaine, avec comme vision sous-jacente celle que chaque personne humaine porte en elle l'image de Dieu et, par conséquent, a droit à la dignité;
>
> — oeuvre en faveur de la justice et de la libération des opprimés; se préoccupe des êtres humains qui se trouvent dans des situations de détresse économique et personnelle;
>
> — croit que la pauvreté, le chômage et l'isolement ne sont pas inévitables.»

3.3.2. En vue des pas à faire dans l'avenir pour participer au processus des actions politiques, on a affirmé à Bratislava que la base de toute action politique devrait être de

> «promouvoir les droits fondamentaux de l'homme dans chaque pays. Certains des droits à défendre sont déjà définis dans des documents tels la Charte sociale du Conseil de l'Europe et le Document final de Helsinki, ainsi que dans les conventions du B.I.T. L'action diaconale devrait soutenir la formation d'un système d'observation de ces droits et entreprendre des actions communes d'urgence en faveur de groupes nationaux ou se joindre à des organisations internationales, si ces droits sont violés.»

3.3.3. En coopération oecuménique et en contact avec le Parlement Européen, avec le Conseil d'Europe et la Commission, les Eglises devraient faire régulièrement pour le public des «récits au sujet de la situation économique et sociale» en Europe sur la base des publications MESOC. En outre, elles devraient marquer les progrès et les faiblesses dans la réalisation d'un aménagement social et d'une culture sociale européens. Les Eglises ont la chance de pouvoir s'appuyer, au sein de leurs propres structures, sur l'engagement et la compétence d'excellents experts et de pouvoir profiter de leurs expériences qu'elles ont faites avec leurs textes d'experts (Denkschriften).

3.3.4. Les églises devraient renforcer et intensifier le travail dans les réseaux existants, comme les programmes «poverty» et HELIOS. Elles devraient en outre proposer de nouveaux modèles de coopération sociale, par exemple dans le domaine d'un échange de jeunes dans le cadre d'une année européenne où l'on peut se qualifier dans les dimensions écologiques et sociales, ainsi que dans les services de la santé et du développement dans le Tiers-Monde. En Europe, l'idée d'une communauté chrétienne de service et de spiritualité a déjà été promulguée d'une façon extraordinaire par les mouvement de Taizé et autres.

3.3.5. Les Eglises devraient continuer et rendre plus concret le processus déjà entamé d'une révision commune de leurs propres ordres juridiques, «processus Lima» au sujet de «baptême, eucharistie, ministère». On a déjà accentué que les Eglises, dans toutes leurs structures et actions officielles, sont assujetties au service de la réconciliation universelle de Dieu dans le monde, et qu'elles travaillent pour que les chrétiens puissent se soumettre au service de la réconciliation. Dans ce sens on lit dans la déclaration Lima en vue de l'Eucharistie:

> «L'Eucharistie embrasse tous les aspects de la vie. Elle est un acte représentatif d'action de grâce et d'offrande au nom du monde entier. La célébration eucharistique présuppose la réconciliation et le partage avec tous, regardés comme frères et soeurs de l'unique famille de Dieu; elle est un constant défi dans la recherche de relations normales au sein de la vie sociale, économique et politique (Mt 5,23 ss; 1Cor. 10,16 ss; 1Cor.11,20-22; Gal. 3,28). Toutes les formes d'injustice, de racisme, de séparation et d'absence de liberté sont radicalement mises au défi quand nous partageons le corps et le sang du Christ. A travers l'Eucharistie, la grâce de Dieu qui renouvelle tout pénètre et restaure la personne humaine et sa dignité. L'Eucharistie entraîne le croyant dans l'évènement central de l'histoire du monde.»

3.3.6. Les conséquences qui découlent du fait que l'Eglise est essentiellement un acte de réconciliation et un service de réconciliation, ne sont ni suffisamment élaborées au niveau théologique, ni assez déployées sur le terrain des perspectives d'action. Dans la «Denkschrift» allemande intitulé *La responsabilité des Eglises pour l'Europe sociale*, les experts concluent ce qui suit:

> «Les perspectives d'une Europe solidaire montrent qu'il reste encore un long et, sans doute, pénible chemin à parcourir. Personne ne s'attend à un développement en ligne droite, bien au contraire les dangers guettent partout: les guerres civiles, les effondrements économiques et la misère des masses. La caractéristique de l'espoir chrétien est de ne tomber ni dans l'optimisme aveugle ni dans le pessimisme résigné, mais de s'orienter aux signes que nous fixe la mission de réconciliation universelle de Dieu dans le monde. C'est pourquoi, les chrétiens, les paroisses chrétiennes et les Eglises sont appelés à se mettre au service de la réconciliation. L'avenir de l'Europe sera fortement influencé par la crédibilité avec laquelle la chrétienté remplira sa propre mission.»

L'ASILE, LE RACISME ET LES MARGINALISÉS AU SEIN DE L'UNION EUROPÉENNE.

LES POSITIONS DES ETATS ET LES NOUVEAUX DÉFIS POUR LES EGLISES

Johan LEMAN

L'Union européenne est en train de se faire. Informellement elle est peut-être déjà plus avancée qu'il ne semble formellement. Les politiques des différentes nations ne suivent pas toujours au même rythme, mais une concertation se fait jour, de plus en plus, au niveau des sociétés civiles.

D'ailleurs, même au niveau des Etats le dialogue fait ses petits progrès.

Et les églises dans tout cela? Pourquoi devraient-elles traîner devant cette concertation commune qui est en train de s'instaurer, surtout lors-qu'il s'agit d'engagements sociaux tellement typiques de leur vocation comme l'accueil des demandeurs d'asile, la lutte contre le racisme et l'amélioration de la situation des marginalisés. Pourquoi les églises devraient-elles refuser d'entrer «à l'européenne» dans cette nouvelle réalité sociale qu'est l'Europe, qui pourrait devenir pour certains aspects de ces problématiques d'une importance primordiale?

Dans ce petit chapitre, nous voulons en quelques traits esquisser la situation actuelle des thèmes indiqués prévalant dans les Etats indivi-duels, premièrement vis-à-vis de l'Union européenne, et complémentai-rement vis-à-vis de leurs propres parlements, pour positionner chaque fois les églises dans ce même débat.

1. L'asile et les réfugiés

1.1. Les Etats vis-à-vis de l'Union européenne

Au niveau des Etats au sein de l'Union européenne, est présente une forte préoccupation de maîtriser et de réduire le plus possible les flux migratoires vers l'Europe qui se servent du droit d'asile (et encore plus, bien sûr, ceux qui se servent des réseaux illégaux internationaux). Cette politique est présente aussi bien au niveau des différents pays qu'au niveau de l'Union européenne dans son ensemble.

Pour le droit d'asile, les éléments qui déterminent le débat politique sont:

a. l'interprétation de la Convention de Genève de 1951;

b. le processus d'harmonisation des procédures suite à l'approbation — en cours — de la Convention de Dublin (1990);

c. l'échange de données entre les différents pays qui participent aux accords de Schengen[1].

Ad a: On doit constater que les différents pays n'interprètent pas nécessairement de la même manière les critères qui sont décisifs pour une application correcte de la *Convention de Genève*. Comment expliquer autrement que les demandeurs d'asile venant de certains pays sont plus facilement reconnus dans un pays de l'Union européenne que dans un autre? Il semble y avoir un certain arbitraire qui fait que les éléments qui semblent convaincants, ou les informations dont on dispose sur les pays de provenance, ne sont pas interprétés de la même manière dans les différents pays de l'Union européenne.

Un débat serein à ce sujet est extrêmement difficile, parce que chaque pays semble vouloir appliquer certains quotas pour la reconnaissance, et cette priorité, qui n'est déjà pas si facile à réaliser, ne laisse pas de temps pour de nouvelles réflexions d'un autre type (voir b)[2].

Ad b: L'harmonisation que l'on a en vue suite à la *Convention de Dublin* est très focalisée sur le délai de temps requis par une procédure et sur le quota final des reconnaissances qui est réalisé. Ceci n'est pas sans impact sur le traitement au cas par cas qui est demandé dans le cadre de la Convention de Genève.

Ad c: L'échange de données dans le cadre des *accords de Schengen* et le fait que les frontières internes devraient en principe disparaître entre les différents pays concernés, devraient mener à une plus grande pression en vue de conserver les différents quotas plus ou moins égaux entre les différents pays de l'Union européenne, sinon tout pays qui arrive à un quota plus élevé risque d'attirer un plus grand nombre de demandeurs d'asile et de devenir l'objet de fortes critiques de la part des pays voisins.

---

[1] Convention d'Application de l'Acccord de Schengen du 14 juin 1985 entre les Gouvernements des Etats de l'Union Economique Benelux, de la République Fédérale d'Allemagne et de la République française, relatif à la suppression graduelle des contrôles aux frontières communes.

[2] Le statut des personnes déplacées est un autre thème qui mérite une réflexion plus mûre au sein de l'Union européenne.

1.2. Les Etats vis-à-vis de leurs propres parlements

Dès à présent les politiques de contrôle appliquées par les différents Etats ne font que rarement l'objet d'un débat parlementaire dans les différents pays, 1. parce que la thématique est très complexe et très ingrate vis-à-vis de l'opinion publique, et 2. parce que la problématique est de toute manière réglée en grande partie au niveau des groupes de travail impliquant les ministres de l'intérieur et les ministres de la justice des différents pays de l'Union européenne surtout dans le cadre des accords de Schengen.

1.3. Les églises devant cette problématique

Sauf quelques rares plaidoyers pour ouvrir un débat sur les politiques migratoires (cfr. Caritas en Belgique), plaidoyers que le monde politique s'efforce de ne pas entendre sinon d'oublier au plus vite, les interventions concrètes des églises semblent se situer exclusivement au niveau des Etats individuels, et surtout dans quatre secteurs:

— l'accueil des demandeurs d'asile dont la demande a été déclarée recevable;
— la régularisation de la situation de certains demandeurs d'asile dont la demande a été refusée et qui sont restés dans le pays;
— les aspects humanitaires pour certaines de ces personnes dont la demande a été refusée et qui restent tout de même dans le pays: p.ex. soins de santé, droit à l'enseignement pour leurs enfants. (Ceci peut aussi être pris en considération pour un illégal tout court.)
— l'accueil d'enfants mineurs non accompagnés par des adultes.

Jusqu'ici ces quatre points d'intérêt ne semblent pas faire l'objet d'actions soutenues de la part des hiérarchies officielles des églises et semblent plutôt soutenues de façon informelle.

Pour les différents points, tant sur la demande d'un débat sur les politiques migratoires que sur les quatre points d'intérêt mentionnés, on n'est pas encore arrivé à des prises de position des églises officielles dans les pays pris individuellement, et ce n'est donc pas non plus le cas au niveau de l'Union européenne.

Points de réflexion au niveau des Eglises:

i le respect strict de la Convention de Genève, y compris: le problème extrêm important et complexe des «personnes déplacées»;
ii la nécessité d'un débat sur les politiques migratoires;

iii l'accueil correct des demandeurs d'asile «recevables»;
iv le problème extrêmement complexe mais inévitable des régularisa-
    tions;
v   les droits des enfants en situation irrégulière (enseignement, ...);
vi les droits aux soins de santé pour les personnes en situation irrégu-
    lière;
vii l'accueil des enfants mineurs non accompagnés.

Remarques:

L'interprétation du respect strict de la Convention de Genève ne peut
être débattue qu'au niveau de l'Union européenne, et d'aucuns jugent
qu'il est plus prudent de ne pas entamer ce débat parce que le résultat
risque d'être pire que la situation actuelle.

Le débat sur les politiques migratoires ne peut être tenu qu'au niveau
de l'Union européenne, mais il est totalement exclu pour le moment.

Le débat sur l'accueil des demandeurs d'asile, le problème des régu-
larisations et le thème des mineurs non accompagnés se situent aux différents niveaux nationaux et sont à mener d'urgence.

Les droits des enfants en situation irrégulière et les droits aux soins de
santé pour les immigrés illégaux pourraient faire l'objet de recommandations au niveau de l'Union européenne.

Les Eglises devraient prioritairement assumer leurs responsabilités
pour les points iii jusqu'à vii compris.

2. Le racisme

2.1. Union européenne vis-à-vis des Etats

— Le Parlement Européen s'est prononcé à plusieurs reprises et par
  plusieurs résolutions contre le racisme et la xénophobie, et cela
  depuis de nombreuses années.

— Le Conseil de l'Europe, auquel les pays de l'Union européenne
  participent parmi d'autres, et aux activités duquel beaucoup d'organisations non-gouvernementales (dont des organisations chrétiennes
  comme Pax Christi International) et le Saint-Siège participent, organise plusieurs réflexions autour du racisme et p.ex. de décembre
  1994 jusqu'à novembre 1995 toute une campagne (à trois niveaux)
  de lutte contre le racisme. Certains pays de l'Union européenne semblent investir plutôt dans des actions contre le racisme soutenues par

le Conseil de l'Europe (Strasbourg) que dans des actions soutenues par l'Union européenne (Bruxelles), ou investissent pour certains aspects plutôt dans le Conseil de l'Europe et pour d'autres plutôt dans l'Union européenne.

Dans cette matière, il y a tendance à inviter des représentants d'une organisation aux grandes réunions de l'autre, pour obtenir au moins un minimum de concertation entre le Conseil de l'Europe et l'Union européenne.

— L'Union européenne a installé une Commission consultative «Racisme et Xénophobie», instituée par le Conseil européen dans ses conclusions de la réunion des 24 et 25 juin 1994, à Corfou. Cette Commission est chargée de «formuler des recommandations, qui seraient dans toute la mesure du possible adaptées aux circonstances nationales et locales, sur une coopération entre les Gouvernements et les différents acteurs sociaux en faveur de la tolérance, de la compréhension et de l'entente avec les étrangers».
Chaque membre de l'Union européenne a un représentant dans cette Commission.

2.2. Les Etats et les institutions nationales

Plusieurs pays de l'Union européenne disposent déjà d'une législation antiraciste et d'institutions nationales qui veillent au respect de cette législation.

Il y a une forte demande de la part des institutions nationales existantes (Royaume-Uni, Pays-Bas, Belgique, Danemark, et plus ou moins équivalentes en France, Allemagne, Espagne) vis-à-vis des pays où de pareilles institutions n'existent pas d'en créer une.

2.3. Les églises vis-à-vis de cette problématique

Comme signalé, il y a une présence du Saint-Siège et de quelques organisations non-gouvernementales surtout au sein du Conseil de l'Europe (Strasbourg).

La présence la plus active auprès des institutions européennes, sous forme d'un lobbying oeuvrant dans le domaine de l'antiracisme, est réalisée par le groupe soutenant la «Ligne de Départ» («Starting Line»).

3. Les marginalisés

En principe, ce point est extrêmement vaste et n'est pas sans ambiguïtés concernant les groupes de populations qu'on peut avoir en vue.

Il semble y avoir un consensus, également parmi les membres de la Commission consultative «Racisme et Xénophobie», que l'exclusion sociale est surtout fonction du manque d'emploi.

Dans ce sens, le «Livre blanc» de la Commission de l'Union européenne, réalisé sous M. Delors, était sans doute un signal très important à haut niveau de la part de l'Union européenne que celle-ci voulait prendre cette problématique en mains.

Il n'est pas démontré que cette approche de lutte contre le chômage jouisse de la même priorité dans chacun des différents pays.

Il me semble que le fondement d'une politique en faveur des marginalisés peut se ramener encore toujours à un double intérêt: une participation la plus généralisée possible au marché de l'emploi et un système de sécurité sociale le plus adéquat possible. Ce double intérêt doit être complété par un droit au logement, garanti par les Constitutions nationales.

Si ces options politiques ne sont pas réalisées, toutes les autres politiques en faveur des marginalisés, me semblent pouvoir n'être que marginales elles-mêmes.

Néanmoins n'oublions pas de signaler que l'Union européenne dispose d'un fonds social (F.S.E.) et d'un Fonds pour les zones moins avancées, et qu'elle dispose d'un Fonds pour le développement de certains quartiers défavorisés dans les grandes villes (EPER).

Ce même principe de Fonds spéciaux (p.ex. fonds pour les villes, fonds pour les exclus …) est également appliqué au niveau national par différents pays.

Il n'en demeure pas moins que le problème le plus aigu se situe presque toujours au niveau de certaines personnes parmi les plus exclues (p.ex. pauvreté générationnelle) que les instances officielles parviennent difficilement à atteindre et pour lesquelles les Eglises ont sans doute un rôle de complément à assumer.

*   *
*

L'aperçu tracé en très grandes lignes est loin d'être complet. Mais être complet n'était pas le but. Plutôt voulions-nous signaler que certaines préoccupations traditionnelles des Eglises sont en train de se ramifier aussi au sein de l'Union européenne et risquent même, dans un certain nombre de cas (comme p.ex. la problématique des demandeurs d'asile), d'y trouver leur résolution majeure.

Il serait regrettable que les grandes idéologies, dont les églises sont des porteurs importants, ne comprennent pas ce glissement qui est en train de se faire et ne commencent pas à se pencher sur ce nouveau défi pour arriver à une concertation et une plateforme adéquates pour y entamer un dialogue avec les technocrates et les politiques, tout en sauvegardant le contact avec leurs bases diversifiées.

WHICH RELATIONSHIPS BETWEEN CHURCHES AND THE EUROPEAN UNION?

ANALYSIS, CHOICES, ARGUMENTS.

Rik TORFS

Introduction

The Conference of 3 February 1995 leads to various conclusions. The variety can be ascribed to the proper style and approach adopted by the authors. Despite this apparent lack of uniformity, a closer look at the texts shows a considerable degree of consent.

But also the conclusions can be looked at in different ways. While the papers presented here tell something about today's church and state system in Europe, they also have an eye on future developments.

In the following final remarks I shall start with an analysis of the existing system of church and state relations in the countries of the European Union. A reflection on future developments entails taking a closer look at the situation we have to deal with today. When a real comparison is engaged, beyond the traditional remark that entirely different local situations cannot be duly brought into connection with each other, remarkable differences but also similarities clearly emerge.

In a second heading I shall try to summarise some of the thoughts presented at the conference. I do so in the form of a scenario instead of simply enumerating separately some possible points of attention.

Finally, I shall briefly try to situate our efforts and the position of churches in the European Union in today's mode of thought on religious freedom and its political translation.

Analysis of Church and State in the European Union Today

Religion and church never were at the heart of European development. Although the European Court of Justice in Luxembourg as well as the Treaty of the European Union, article F, have developed the legal principle of the common constitutional traditions of the Member States, church and state relations in the European Union remain mutually very different, in each case a result of national history and tradition.

The interventions and discussions at the conference have shown however that to focus on traditional national models might be too easy an approach and could dangerously hide the real issues.

In his contribution, Silvio Ferrari describes the traditional classification of church-state systems in Western Europe which makes a distinction between three groups, as outdated. A division into (a) separation systems, (b) concordatarian systems and (c) national church systems is no longer adequate. As Ferrari states, this approach over-emphasises the formal side of the relationships. It tends to hide what is really at stake. If one wants to do more than throwing up a façade, a closer analysis is necessary.

That is what Ferrari attempts to do in his further analysis, where he tries to discover a common pattern of church-state relations in Western Europe. He sees three points, namely (a) at the individual level the neutral attitude of the State towards the confession of people, (b) at the collective level the outlining of a religious sub-sector inside the public sector, (c) at both levels the limited role of the state which is only entitled to make the rules of the game. This pattern, proposed by Ferrari, fits much better with reality than the traditional formal discussions do. But, as the author recognises, it does not solve all the problems at once.

In order to work out the three principles, it is necessary to make use of a certain number of legal terms and notions. Among these, the notion internal autonomy of the religious community is different from country to country. It is in fact an open notion which is, for example, interpreted much more extensively in Germany than in Spain. Moreover, many key notions of the church and state system remain largely influenced by an underlying christian range of thought. Further clarification of the problem or at least the awareness of it seems to be necessary. Otherwise, the façade hiding the real discussion could be changed from the artificial formal division to the abstract elusiveness of legal notions. What one reads in this field is not sufficient on its own, it can hide a surprising variety of presuppositions and interpretations that slowly grow.

What is true for the general classification of the various systems and for the real meaning of the legal notions employed, is also present at another level, namely that of the demarcation between topics related to church and state issues and those foreign to that domain. Maybe the practical approach in this field remains a little too classic. For instance, what is today's relevance of the (otherwise blameworthy) prohibition of a religious marriage not preceded by a civil one, in France, Germany or Belgium? It is a typical problem of the past, of an era in which church and state were competing over the control over the registry of births, deaths and marriages. On the other hand, more modern problems often are not seen as having to do with the relationship between church and state. Sophie van Bijsterveld rightly observes that, at first sight, European institutions do not infringe on the national constitutional church and state arrangements. But, as she remarks, a closer look at things, shows that national church and state problems are involved in a wide variety of areas ranging from tax law to labour law, from data protection to mass media law. One could even say that for many people these topics are the real issues of modern society.

So, the demarcation between church-state problems and the other areas is a third field in which we have to avoid throwing up a façade. The recognition of the relevance of a certain dossier for church and state relationships is a first and indispensable step before the discussion can be started. But decisions and demarcations in this field are often maid implicitly. And in this regard, ungoing secularisation undoubtedly plays an important role. While in defining open notions such as religion or public order, both traditional elements of the church-state discussion, christian ideas implicitly continue to prevail, the contrary is true concerning the demarcation of areas, as well as the fact of recognising that a problem could at least partially be related to church and state relations. In the latter discussion, the underlying train of thought today is not christian but thoroughly secular: for many people, the role of religion is not an obvious component of discussion in society.

In conclusion of this heading I wish to remark the following. Reflecting about church and state in the European Union starts with a deeper analysis of the existing system, respecting national church and state structures. In three different areas should we look at things carefully and try to unmask appearances: (a) in the field of general structures: the traditional division of European systems of church and state does no longer fit, new common standards have to be developed; (b) in the field of legal notions: key terms such as autonomy, religion, public order are just open terms and are by no means a guarantee for a uniform interpretation; (c) in the field of the demarcation-line between church and state-problems and other topics: implicit choices tend to restrict the relevance of church and state-discussion for the large options in society.

Points of Interest for the Future

How can we possibly deal with the future juridical position of churches within the European Union? Successively, six points of interest should be taken into consideration.

The first question concerns the position of the churches themselves. It is important to point out how they should deal with the upcoming importance of the European legislation. Of course, they can focus either on the content of their message or on their own structural position within the system. Of both aspects, the content is without any doubt the more important one. A generous approach of Europe, deliberately not focusing on one's own possible power but on the message the churches proclaim, should be an absolute priority. This idea is clearly present in the essays written by Johan Leman, Theodor Strohm and Britta von Schubert. The fact that these authors deal with the issue illustrates clearly that such a danger exists. At the same time, the former does not mean that a more structural approach, which tends to strenghten the churches' position in the European Union, should be neglected. It is perfectly possible to combine taking care of the content while paying attention to good structures. However prof. Strohm on many occasions quite rightly said and wrote that churches cannot use their taking notice of a structural position as an excuse for defending their own aspirations to power.

This first question concerning these structures and the churches leads to another one: who should take the initiative for aiming at better structures for the churches? Should it be taken by politicians? By representatives of strong churches in certain countries? By minority churches as well? Here again a simultaneous approach should be recommended. One can, at the same time, (a) make the subject politically debatable without involving all the churches in the discussion in the first instance, (b) try to stimulate the inner church discussion and (c) help minority churches to be alert to the importance European Law could also present to them in a rather near future.

Besides, the question whether churches should aspire to a structurally comfortable position in the European Union does not exclusively depend on them. Indeed, the state has to accept such a partnership and should acknowledge the need or desirability of a structural position for churches. This could possibly lead to a larger debate in society concerning the role of the churches in Europe. Francis Messner pointed this out for France, by correctly stating that certain apparent church problems such as the juridic position of catholic schools and the dismissal of the former bishop of Evreux, Msgr. Gaillot, are also a subject of intense dis-cussions by non-believers. The latter often turn out to take more than a superficial interest in topics of this kind. Will the state allow a structural position for the organised churches the way they operate today, with all the consequences this status might entail? Or will it put under pressure indirectly inner church structures by showing a certain reluctance towards an official position for churches?

In this very framework, one has to be aware of the fact that, in a num-ber of quite concrete debates held today in State law and in civil society, churches are largely absent, or at least poorly represented. Leman gave a perfect illustration of this phenomenon, when it comes to the ungoing debate on racism and the multicultural society. The role of the church in these matters tends to be rather marginal. It does not include a consider-able role in political decision making. Quite often, churches have only to face the results of the policies decided upon by others. They can only try to go along with its consequences as well as possible.

Again from the angle of the state, a third and last question concerns the difference between churches and other international bodies in society. Although churches could rely upon international and national legislation to protect their position in society, it is not sure that, in a somewhat more distant future, their special position will be maintained. Secularisation weakened the broader attention for what might make the difference between religions and other intermediate bodies. This leads to questions like: why should churches be privileged in comparison to other associations?

This concludes my remarks on the possible structural position of the churches in the European Union. While dealing with it, one should look at both sides of the picture. While for churches the content of their message is crucial and the active interest of all churches to build a solid relationship with the European Union seems to be required, the point of view of the State should also be taken into account. The latter might have some reasons to remain sceptical towards a structural position for the churches in the European Union indeed. This is an element of the discussion churches have to be aware of. They can ask themselves ques-tions about which way to be followed, a structural one or some other approach. But in case they make a choice for a structural approximation, state authorities are not necessarily likely to welcome this request with open arms.

The second question we have to deal with here goes one step further. In case a structural position for churches is believed to be desirable, which concrete way can be chosen? In the text presented by Heidrun Tempel, three possible solutions are offered. One can make use of (a) the way of fundamental rights, (b) the concordatarian approach and (c) the way of cooperation. Here again, simple choices should be avoided at any price. The pursuing of one approach does not necessarily exclude all the others. At the same time, an option which eagerly focuses on all possible ways at once might sound a little optimistic or could be indicative of some hesitancy in pointing out one's strategy. One has to move prudently, taking advantage of the right opportunity, making use of the best qualified people one can get. Options cannot be made without taking into consideration their practical impact. For that reason, the three possible ways shown by Tempel need some closer examination.

So, the third question concerns the first way which leads to granting the churches an acceptable structural position in the European Union: the way of fundamental rights. Article 9 of the European Convention for Human Rights is at the basis of a certain problem in this field. It tends to protect more generously individual religious freedom rather than its collective counterpart. This might at least partly be due to historic motives. But one cannot deny that organised religions were not primarily aimed at in article 9, ECHR. Anyway, what can be done concretely in order to stimulate the human rights-approach as a possible tool of improvement for the position of churches in the European Union? Making abstraction from some more sophisticated manoeuvres, one could try to convince the European Union to sign the ECHR. As such this appears to be a rather isolated initiative, quite easy to manage and to control as a possible project to strive to.

The fourth question deals with the desirability of a concordatarian approach. A concordat is an almost mythical tool in order to stabilise church and state relationships. It functions well in a certain number of countries. For instance, the successful revision in Italy of the concordat, as it was agreed upon in 1984, was a clear proof of the concordatarian technique not being necessarily a juridical technique of the past, that is, of times in which the societas perfecta-idea propagated by the catholic church suited wonderfully well with the concordat as a juridical institution. Today, there are reasons for concordats being the subject of a revival. In other words, they could be a good illustration of trends in modern society which see the government engage in a sincere dialogue with dynamic forces active within its territory.

However, although the concordat remains within a given context a possible useful technique to deal properly with church and state relations, one can hardly see it as the best way to juridically organise a structural position for churches within the European Union. Already on technical grounds, problems do occur. Firstly, the international legal position of concordats today is challenged much more than before. Secondly, how could one imagine a concordat between partners who are not mutually independent? In Denmark, for example, as Gerhard Robbers quite correctly pointed out during the discussions, a clear distinction between the two possible partners cannot be made. Thirdly, the political and psychological difficulties present themselves as even more important. Not every church would be in favour of a concordat, which would not necessarily be beneficial to all possible religious movements. Moreover, in the hypothesis of a concordat between the European Union and the catholic church, how would the reactions be in countries such as for instance the United Kingdom or Denmark, countries having an established church in their system? Probably, the obvious technical, political and psychological difficulties will convince even ardent principal supporters of the concordatarian technique that, in a European context, it is not the right way to choose.

Of course there are less radical possibilities available. The fifth question is linked with these other forms of possible cooperation between church and state. Which possibilities could be taken into consideration in this respect? Here, several ways show a certain value. One of these might be the insertion of some provision concerning the churches' position in a future European constitution. However, this goal lies rather far away: a European constitution will be a tough aim to achieve.

More realistic could be the demand for a legal basis for churches in the European Treaty. A provision focusing on churches is maybe not urgently necessary, but it could be an important sign of mutual respect between the churches and the European institutions.

Anyway, what should such a provision look like? Or, even before answering this question, should it be a provision? One could argue that a provision expressing a statement of principle does not fit perfectly in the logical line of thinking of European law. For instance, one cannot solemnly guarantee that existing church and state relations will always be respected, when at the same time, a lot of new European legislation is issued, possibly influencing indirectly the church-state-relationship as they are established in the member states.

However, if a provision on the churches were accepted, what should it look like? Here again several possibilities are conceivable and open for discussion. One could focus on the safeguarding of the existing situation in the member states. Such an approach, and more specifically such a way of formulating things, looks somewhat defensive, although this is not necessarily the case. If one interprets *safeguard* as keeping things as they are on the national level, then its defensive significance can hardly be denied. On the other hand, *safeguard* could also have a more European-inspired meaning, in the sense of the common European pattern as Ferrari pointed out. This could lead to the safeguarding of what is essential and positive, meanwhile leaving out several often rather outdated points of the legislation which do not fit well in the common European pattern.

Another possibility consists of mentioning the church and state relations as they exist in the member states, without using the word *safeguard* and the rather negative connotations the latter could entail.

In both instances, in case one makes use of the term *safeguard* and in case one does not, referring to churches in a provision of the Treaty reminds the legislator of the fact that European law could possibly affect church and state relations in the member states and that, if it does, some balancing between all concerned appears to be unavoidable.

This concludes some remarks concerning the concrete juridic organisation of cooperation between the European Union and the churches in European law.

Taking into consideration all the elements evoked under the title *Points of Interest for the Future*, one comes to a sixth question, which focuse on concrete steps which could be undertaken. It is a summary of the heading as a whole. When dealing with the juridic position of churches in the European Union, four questions have to be asked in succession:

(a) Should there be any structural and juridic position of churches in European law? This problem can be analysed from the point of view of some or from the point of view of all churches and religious movements. It can be considered from the perspective of some or all member states, and ultimately also from the standpoint of the European Union itself.

(b) If the first question is answered in a positive way, if a structural position of churches in the European Union appears to be desirable, then which are the techniques one should or could make use of? Tempel enumerates the human rights-approach, the concordat and other forms of cooperation. These are the techniques at a macro-level.

(c) Each of those techniques can be elaborated in various ways. Several options remain open. Their achievement takes place by means of techniques at a micro-level. They include questions such as: which forms of cooperation are possible? How could the juridic position of churches be formulated in the European Treaty?

(d) The last step is a tactical one. Not every move or approach which appears to be theoretically conceivable, is also possible. Here the question rises: who should introduce which solution at what moment?

A healthy approach of church and state-relationships in the European Union certainly includes those four steps, namely the question dealing with choices of principle, the technical macro-approach, the technical micro-approach, the tactical elaboration of the options finally taken.

Towards a Broader Context

Up to here, two discussion areas have been dealt with. Firstly, I briefly described the existing situation of churches in the European Union. As Ferrari pointed out, traditional patterns turn out to be outdated and superficial. A new approach is proposed. Meanwhile, one has to take care of legal terminology: open notions might hide a different approach under the umbrella of an uniformous terminology. Finally, one has to be aware of the continuous demarcation line between church and state.

The second title dealt with the concrete results we reached at the Brussels meeting of 3 February 1995. From political choices over technical macro and micro questions to tactical points of attention, a wide range of possible positions of churches in the European Union was covered.

It would be possible to finish this concluding article at this point, but I cannot resist taking the opportunity to formulate some personal ideas on the future position of churches in the European Union.

I can imagine — and I can to a certain point sympathise with the idea — that some people might be sceptical concerning a possible juridic position of churches in the European Union. This scepticism could be given a more or less scientific basis on two different levels.

On a first level, one could argue that, as church and state matters remain under the competency of member states, there is no need for any kind of action regarding legislation at the level of the European Union.

On a second level, this practical argument could be supported by a more fundamental one. Indeed, is a legal provision concerning churches really a valuable aim to strive for? One could argue that the simple general recognition of freedom of religion should do. By acknowledging this freedom and doing no more than that, other possible problems can be avoided: (a) no religion is awarded a privileged position, (b) together with freedom, equality among all denominations is automatically realised. Moreover, the inflation of legislative acts has to stop somewhere, thus, why not here, occasionally at the level of the juridic position of churches in the European Union?

Although the limpid character of this reasoning is not without attraction, I dare say that at both the first and the second level it can be subject of serious criticism.

Of course, the first argument, as such, is true. The European Union does not deal with the juridic position of churches. On the one hand, one could see this as a recognition of each country's historically grown situation. On the other hand, one could look at it in another way: the fact that Europe does not cover this topic also means that in a secularised society it is not considered to be a priority. Anyway, the fact that the juridic position of churches is not dealt with, entails as a consequence that the whole topic remains out of the picture. In issuing new legislation — and we have seen that at this level modern church and state problems might indirectly emerge — the legislator seldom bears the churches' position clearly in mind. This has as a consequence that no implicit balancing takes places between the aims of the new legislation and the interest of the churches. The simple presence of some juridic tool at the European level, recognising the churches or their role, could avoid a one-sided approach when it comes to problems which fall under European competence, such as data protection or broadcasting.

The second argument is, as I mentioned, more fundamental and therefore deserves a more fundamental approach as well. Is it really true that, not focusing on the churches' position but merely proclaiming religious freedom, leads to more equality among religions and to a higher degree of freedom? For both questions the answer is, as far as I am concerned, a negative one.

Firstly, the equality argument, very valuable as such, does not seem to work out perfectly well in concrete situations. While analysing on 12-13 January 1995, with a group of Western experts, the draft of 22 November 1994 of a new Russian Federation Federal Law on the Freedom of Conscience and Religious Organizations, a very interesting question, relating to the Russian situation but with broader implications, occurred. It could be summarised as follows. Should the new law establish full equality among all religions active or possibly active in Russia, or should it give a certain juridic preference to the orthodox church? At first sight, and certainly looking at it from a fundamental angle, the answer seems to be easy. Natural sympathy goes to equality, as it often goes to constructions characterised by the purity of their approach. But a closer look at the problem makes things less simple. Indeed, if total equality were legally established, there would be a risk that judges, most of them belonging to the orthodox church, might limit the scope of activity of all religions but the orthodox, by making use, for doing so, of notions such as "the fundamentals of the constitutional regime", "morals", "health" and even "misanthropy", among other criteria of exeption mentioned in the articles 3 and 5 of the draft. On the other hand, a moderate form of friendly treatment in favour of the orthodox church, entailing for instance financial advantages or the recognition of a certain role in public life, could probably satisfy the orthodox and could be accompanied, at the same time, by very strong guarantees for the complete freedom of every religion, its faithful and its activities. In other words: by accepting a certain, well balanced inequality, a basic freedom for every religion could be guaranteed. Ultimately, although there is some formal inequality, the second approach may lead to a higher degree of real equality. It removes the reason for undermining religious freedom indirectly, for instance by jurisprudencial techniques.

Of course, this Russian case remains very Russian, but it illustrates that the absence of any legislative attention for church and state matters does not automatically lead to a higher degree of equality among religions. The latter goal remains of course very important, but can probably be better achieved through a pragmatic approach which relies upon culture and tradition than by well-sounding abstract principles, sometimes equally impressive as they are naïve.

But even freedom as such is not necessarily served by leaving out any church and state legislation, or by focusing merely on religious freedom as such. In the late twentieth century, in the West, almost no initiatives, be it an idealistic one such as Greenpeace or Médecins sans Frontières, be it the churches, can survive without healthy structures supporting their concrete activities. Probably it is not absolutely necessary to give churches and other organisations money, but at least they should be juridically well enough equipped in order to be able to raise it themselves. This is particularly true for minoritarian churches, which are not able to rely upon influencial members or upon indirect support by government policy. Perhaps it is not a popular statement in our times of scepticism towards both power structures and organisations in general, but even religion is not merely a matter of ideas. In today's public speech, the message of religion and its structural organisation are too easily set apart. Politicians of various political parties not seldom underline the value of christian ideas for society. However, those ideas do not emerge on their own, starting from zero. Someone has to be the one who formulates the idea. And this person, even when being rather sceptical to the church-life of his time, functions within or in interaction with the very church he belongs or belonged to. One can hardly make friendly statements on christian ideas, while at the same time completely rejecting the church as an institution. Of course, *omnis comparatio claudicat*. But a reasoning as mentioned above could be compared to a statement of someone saying that he loves the branches of a tree but that, as far as he is concerned, its roots are of no use whatsoever. Real freedom is only possible when both liberties are awarded and their real application guaranteed. All this of course cannot be meant to support privileges of the past, but only to be of practical use in the juridic life of modern democracies. In his times, a somewhat forgotten person, Vladimir I. Lenin, turned out to be sceptical towards juridical rights and liberties granted to citizens, arguing that the poor had other problems to deal with. He was right: a theoretical proclamation of liberties is not sufficient and might even be a sign of provocation in case taking advantage of it remains practically impossible. Lenin's ideas could, *mutatis mutandis*, be applied on today's church and state problems: as far as churches are concerned, religious freedom is an idle concept if it lacks the opportunity to develop its own policy based upon solid structures. Particularly for poor or weak churches or religious movements which only can rely upon themselves, such a structural approach offers much more guarantees than the simple but easy affirmation which solemnly announces that religious freedom exists.

LIST OF PARTICIPANTS

PARTICIPANTS AU COLLOQUE

Sophie VAN BIJSTERVELD, Chargé de cours à la Katholieke Universiteit Brabant, Tilburg

Hubert DEMEESTER, Professeur à la K.U.Leuven. Sécrétaire-général du Centre Interdiocésain à Bruxelles

Filip DEWALLENS, Avocat, Assistant à la K.U.Leuven

Silvio FERRARI, Professeur à l'Université de Milan

Keith JENKINS, Sécrétaire-général de la Commission Européenne Oecuménique pour Eglise et Société (EECCS), Bruxelles

Ward KENNES, Assistant à la K.U.Leuven. Directeur adjoint JRS (Jesuit Refugee Service)

Hans-Joachim KIDERLEN, Président du Consistoire de la Kirchenprovinz Sachsen, Magdeburg

Johan LEMAN, Professeur à la K.U.Leuven. Directeur du Centre pour l'égalité des chances, Bruxelles

Francis MESSNER, Directeur de Recherches au CNRS, Strasbourg

Gerhard ROBBERS, Professeur à l'Université de Trèves

Britta von SCHUBERT, Diakoniewissenschaftliches Institut, Université de Heidelberg

Theodor STROHM, Professeur à l'Université de Heidelberg

Heidrun TEMPEL, Directeur du Bureau de l'Eglise Evangélique d'Allemagne (EKD), Bruxelles

Rik TORFS, Professeur à la K.U.Leuven

ORIENTALISTE, KLEIN DALENSTRAAT 42, B-3020 HERENT